HISTORIC HOUSES
of the HUDSON RIVER VALLEY
1663–1915

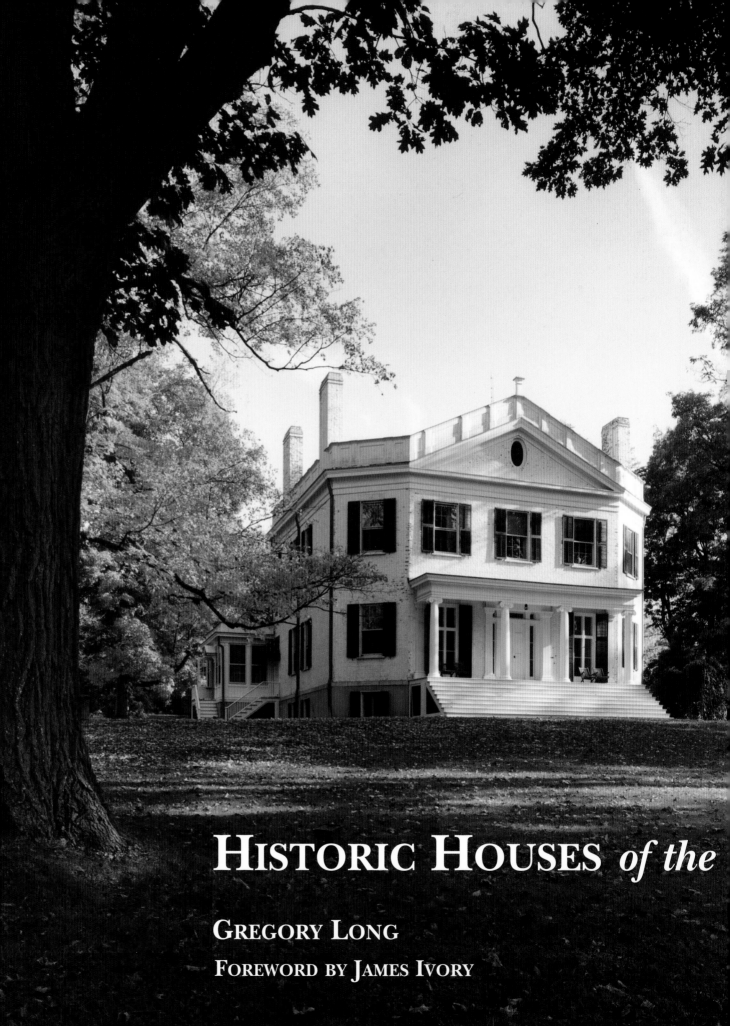

HISTORIC HOUSES *of the*

GREGORY LONG

FOREWORD BY JAMES IVORY

HUDSON RIVER VALLEY   1663–1915

RIZZOLI
NEW YORK

PRESERVATION LEAGUE OF NEW YORK STATE

First published in the United States of America in 2004 by
Rizzoli International Publications, Inc.
300 Park Avenue South
New York, NY 10010
www.rizzoliusa.com

In association with the Preservation League of New York State

This publication is supported by a grant from
Furthermore, the publication program of the J. M. Kaplan Fund

ISBN-13: 978-0-8478-2656-8
LCCN: 2004104804

FRONT COVER: *Edgewater, Dutchess County*
BACK COVER: *Schuyler Mansion, Albany*
TITLEPAGE: *Jacob Rutsen Van Rensselaer House, Columbia County*

Designed by Abigail Sturges

Printed in China

2009 2010 / 10 9 8 7 6 5 4

Contents

Foreword

The Hudson River Valley's hold on us, its attraction for us, is out of all proportion with everything about it except its evident beauty, which from the first stirrings of an artistic consciousness in this country has been celebrated by painters and writers. Europeans have long been struck by the Hudson and its valley, comparing it most often to the Rhineland, but the region's history, in which their compatriots long ago played prominent roles, has yet to be presented (one might say "produced") in the thorough-going fashion of New England, Virginia, Charleston, or parts of the deep South.

The Hudson Valley somehow remains obscure, even uncharted, and yet its attractions are an easy drive from New York City; the scenery glimpsed from the river-side tracks during a train ride to Albany is beautiful at all times of the year and in every kind of weather. The journey presents the same views that entranced the Hudson River School painters more than a century ago, almost unchanged: bluffs and stone escarpments rising up from mostly undeveloped shoreline, still smothered in dense vegetation that looks steamily tropical in the summer, giving way to the grandest vistas of water and sky and high hills—crowned sometimes with what looks like a castle—which, as you go north, prepare the way for the Catskill Mountains. There are grand sunsets too, and mighty cloud formations. As the river zigs and zags, the alternating lights and shadows that struck painters like Frederic Edwin Church will also delight the responsive traveler. From the windows of the train in mid-winter the river is like a frozen sea, with slabs of ice flung up by ice-breakers into weird formations suggesting another romantic painter, Caspar David Friedrich. As the writer John Reed has pointed out in his excellent book, *The Hudson River Valley*, the Hudson is a great river first by the grace of nature.

The counties and landscapes lining the river, very generally comprising the Hudson River Valley, are rich with historic houses of all types. Some of them seem to be monuments to pride and power, others to a feeling for beauty, while still others may seem like monuments to eccentricity. The selection in this book begins with the earliest and most primitive houses remaining and finishes just before World War I. These are by no means all grand or especially overbearing houses; they come in all shapes, sizes, and degrees of formality. But many were once the homes of the Hudson Valley's landed aristocracy, the original settlers of this part of New York State. So a whiff of their old autocratic command over the region and its houses may still be sensed— if only in the many redolent sounding place names, mostly Dutch or grandly English (and even Scottish), that dot today's upstate roadmaps.

The Hudson Valley was divided up in the late seventeenth century by a number of enterprising Dutch and British land speculators who were given the title "Patroon" or "Lord of the Manor" over their lands by their respective kings. These lands were sometimes vast and lay on both sides of the river. It was the European feudal system carried to the New World. The populations of these manors were mostly pioneer tenant farmers, small tradesmen, free and enslaved Blacks, and Native Americans, who called the Hudson "Oiogue," meaning the beautiful river. The manors were, moving north from Manhattan, Philipse, Van Cortlandt, Livingston, and the largest—and grandest for aristocratic pretensions—Van Rensselaer. These American lords and their descendants dominated upstate politics and business affairs until the early nineteenth century, and to a large extent the society of New York City for a good deal longer, until they were overshadowed by a new generation of tycoons who tried to emulate and then outdo them—the Astors and Vanderbilts and other such grandees.

What legacy did these Lords of the Manor leave behind that the interested traveler to upstate New York might seek? They did relatively little to change the world. Unlike the Boston "Brahmins," who came from a resoundingly mercantile tradition, these American aristocrats—the "River Folk"—produced few serious writers or artists, no great reformers (except Franklin Delano Roosevelt), and few inventors. Their influence as framers of Colonial and post-Revolutionary law lessened as time went by, unlike that of their counterparts in Virginia, where descendants of the earliest plantation owners are still very active in national and state affairs. But they left something else instead: a legacy of beautiful houses, enchantingly situated along what is still a mostly unsullied river, and of these, the houses of the Livingstons and their friends are the most numerous.

This book has been created, and is published, in association with the Preservation League of New York State, a non-profit organization with which I have been associated for many years. No group knows better the current challenges to our historic buildings and landscapes here in the Empire State. And no group does more to help the people and towns of New York address those challenges. It is to everyone engaged today in the business of saving our visual heritage and protecting our built environment that the League dedicates this survey of Hudson River houses.

JAMES IVORY
Claverack
Columbia County, New York
January 2004

Introduction

The story of domestic architecture in the Hudson River Valley between 1663 and 1915 is inextricably tied to New York's unique cultural and social history, from the Dutch Colonial period, through the surprisingly late dissolution of the manorial system in 1846, until the local career of Franklin Delano Roosevelt as a New York State Assemblyman before World War I. Celebrated for its awe-inspiring landscape; for providing the setting for so much Revolutionary activity; for the Hudson River School of painting; for its role in building Colonial commerce and leading nineteenth-century America to great industrial and financial power, the Hudson River Valley is not usually understood as being an open-air museum of historic houses. Yet that is what it is.

There are few other regions in America that provide as rich and clear a display of stylistic change and development in domestic architecture through three centuries as this beautiful river valley. Recorded history began here in 1609, and it has been both dramatic and consequential. Along the way, the Hudson River Valley has become home to a remarkable sequence of important historic houses, more than in many other regions because of the Valley's early settlement and because of its two centers of commerce, finance, and wealth—New York City and Albany. Both were established early on as centers of Dutch trade, and the financial capital they created, even before the War of Independence, built and has maintained for centuries many Hudson Valley houses.

In 1942, Harold Donaldson Eberlein and Cortlandt Van Dyke Hubbard published their important book, *Historic Houses of the Hudson Valley*, with its two hundred beautiful photographic plates, short descriptions of scores of historic buildings, large format, and enticing maps. At least two generations of travelers, old-house enthusiasts, and architectural historians have depended upon this beautiful compilation as they roamed up and down this magnificent valley. There have been a few other books since then, and Eberlein and Hubbard is now quite out of date, but never since has the geographical, stylistic, and social scope of this treasured set of houses been so movingly portrayed. In this current survey, Eberlein and Hubbard's book has been a touchstone and inspiration.

The goal of this project is to trace the development of domestic architectural style through the stories of, and with the most up-to-date information about, 39 houses built across 252 years. It begins in 1663, with the Dutch vernacular style, the earliest example of which is the Bronck house in Greene County, and ends in 1915, with the Colonial Revival style as seen at Springwood, the Franklin Delano Roosevelt house in Dutchess County. This survey stops short of World War I, the coming of European Modernism, and the story of twentieth-century American architecture. All the major architectural styles of this long time-period are included, although it is beyond the scope of the project to illustrate all of the ideas of the later nineteenth century. Included are houses from the southern, central, and northern sections of the Valley, from Bronx to Saratoga Counties, and houses on both sides of the river. Although there are several well-known mansions in this group, the bias is toward the smaller, vernacular houses—some of which are museums and open to the public, and some of which are private residences. It has been rewarding to meet the curators of the twenty-five houses that are public museums, as well as the owners of the fourteen private houses, to sift through old documents and books for the most accurate and useful information, and to make new discoveries like the extensive work of the designer-builder Nathaniel Lockwood Jr. of Dutchess County.

It is not more than 150 miles from the southernmost of these houses to the northernmost. An avid traveler can easily visit at least three house museums in one day, starting, for example, with a visit to an eighteenth-century Dutch house in Kinderhook, then driving up to Albany to see a major Georgian house of 1761, and doubling back down to Annandale-on-Hudson before dark to tour an important Federal house of 1804. A map of the river valley identifying house museums is included to encourage this kind of self-organized study tour.

Most of the house museums are decorated in period style, many with fine New York furniture, so there is much to be learned about the decorative arts as well as architecture and American history. Many of the museums also have historic grounds and gardens curated by professional staffs. Beginning in the mid-nineteenth century, in the era of the writer and tastemaker Andrew Jackson Downing, the design of domestic landscapes became of great interest and significance to New Yorkers, and many of these landscapes are intact today.

A word about the organization of the houses into seven historical periods. These divisions are, of course, somewhat arbitrary, as one sees trends and development over time, the gradual filtering in of new ideas. Alas, there are no crisp dates when periods end and begin—there is too much overlapping, too much complexity. The houses are grouped into periods, not in order to pigeonhole each building, but to add to the reader's understanding by providing interesting comparisons of architectural characteristics and by encouraging the reader to think about domestic architecture in terms of the history of style.

In spite of all we can learn and the pleasure we can derive from these wonderful buildings, historic preservation is no longer simply about old houses. Today it is about public policy concerning historic roadways, farm and landscape conservation, affordable housing in aging cities, and adaptive reuse in many situations, including main streets in communities that are not affluent. It is also about good but difficult new ideas such as wind farms, which capture a clean and renewable source of energy even as they alter historic viewsheds. As complex as all of these new concerns have made our lives, the buildings illustrated here, which were for the most part saved by much earlier generations of historic preservationists, remain among our greatest cultural treasures and speak to all who care about the history of our country and our art and architecture.

CHAPTER 1

THE EARLIEST HOUSES: DUTCH VERNACULAR STYLE

The pre-Revolutionary Dutch houses of the Hudson River Valley are the earliest buildings in New York State. The Dutch controlled the region from 1609, when Henry Hudson sailed up the "North River," as he named the Hudson, and traders soon began to come to the Hudson Valley for furs. By 1621, the Dutch West India Company had been formed to promote trade and settlement, and "New Netherland" was established. Dutch rule lasted only until 1664, when Peter Stuyvesant surrendered in New Amsterdam to the British forces sent by King Charles II and his brother the Duke of York. Dutch style and culture lasted much longer, however, and Dutch construction techniques and taste can be seen in houses built as late as the nineteenth century.

The first Dutch Colonial houses were primitive wooden structures, and they are all lost. Many stone and brick houses from the seventeenth and eighteenth centuries survive, concentrated around Albany (known to the Dutch as Beverwyck) and Kingston (the Dutch Wiltwyck). These early houses are to some extent similar to those in other colonies, and a clear "Dutch style" is not easy to define, but many New York houses do share several characteristics. They are usually only one room or two, each measuring about twenty feet square and often with divided "Dutch" doors, and they have full cellars with dry-laid stone walls. Roofs are steep, typically single-pitched rather than gambrel.

The stone houses among them have load-bearing walls with heavy joists spanning the distance between them. In contrast, brick houses have a timber frame structure with the brick applied as an exterior skin. The heavy posts and beams are always exposed on the interior. Ceilings are not plastered, leaving joists and floor planks visible. A few small casement windows admit light and air. Fireplaces are open, consisting of a hearth and a chimney with a hood to catch the smoke. At the top of an enclosed stairway would be a garret, or two levels of garret, generally for storage, as the Dutch preferred to sleep on the ground floor.

Inspired by Northern European models, Dutch vernacular houses such as these are found only in the Hudson Valley, on Long Island, and in New Jersey. Contemporary houses in the other colonies were generally based on seventeenth-century English models. Dutch houses are iconic in this part of America, having fired the imaginations of nineteenth-century literary figures such as Washington Irving as well as builders of modern "Dutch Colonial" houses. Scores of original Dutch-built houses in counties such as Albany, Dutchess, and Ulster are still in use today as private homes, testimony to their sturdy construction, their livability, and the longevity of Dutch culture in the region.

Luykas Van Alen House
Kinderhook, Columbia County, 1737

This brick structure illustrates many characteristics of the Dutch vernacular. In the older section, on the left, there are two rooms, each with an exterior door and a fireplace. There is a stone foundation and cellar, and a garret under the steep roof. The interiors are especially fine, with smooth-planed beams and joists with corbels for extra support. The house is decorated with Delftware and handsome eighteenth-century furniture.

The Bronck Museum

Coxsackie, Greene County, 1663–1738

The stone house built in 1663 by Pieter Bronck (c. 1617–1669) about twenty miles south of Albany is the oldest extant dwelling in the Hudson Valley. With three later additions, it is now part of a curious and picturesque complex known as the Bronck House. The house also has one freestanding dependency, three barns, and outbuildings that form a real farmstead, an authentic group of buildings native to the site, at least one of which has endured for 340 years.

Of Swedish extraction, Pieter Bronck, a brewer and tavern-keeper in Albany, is thought to have been the cousin of Jonas Bronck, who had a farm north of the Harlem River, in the area now called The Bronx. By 1661, Pieter Bronck was deeply in debt. Desiring a new life in the country, he sold his tavern and brewery to buy this farm, which was perhaps also a fur-trading outpost. Debt-ridden as he may have been, he did not give up his town connections, and he and his wife always maintained a house in Albany as well.

Bronck's one-room farmhouse is a typical Dutch vernacular building. Approximately twenty feet square, it has load-bearing stone walls, large floor joists spanning the width of the house, a high garret above, and a stone-floored cellar. This building is made of local gray limestone with brick arches over the windows; stone is an unusual material for this early date, but it would have been easily available from the stream that flows behind the house.[1] The steep roof is now shingled, but was originally perhaps thatch (found in abundance in the nearby swamps) or planks. The house originally had an open fireplace. This smoky system was improved by later alteration to the English-style firebox (with jambs), probably in the eighteenth century. About that time, a wood-paneled wall with built-in cupboards was installed.

*Bronck family furniture of
the 1800s occupies this Dutch
vernacular room.*

Two structures have been added to the original building. The wing to the west, consisting of a hallway with an open stair (a later improvement) and a large room used now as a dining room, is constructed of load-bearing, limestone rubble walls, similar to those of the 1663 building. The construction method suggests that it was built in the late seventeenth century, but the 1981 Historic Structure Report dates it to the late eighteenth century.[2]

A more formal brick house to the north, built in 1738 by Leendert Bronck, Pieter's grandson, sets the tone for the whole complex. On the front, this building has two doors and two windows, a pair of shed dormers with brick flanking walls, and a curious double porch with a tiny bridge connecting its two halves. Just as "Dutch" as the earlier part, it is much larger and higher, and has a fine design. The structure is different from the stone houses, but equally traditional in the Dutch vernacular: H-frame post-and-beam construction faced in brick. A small brick hyphen connects the 1738 house to the earlier stone buildings.

The earliest room in the house,
c. 1663.

PAGES 20–21: *The house from*
the back, across Coxsackie Creek.
The Dutch barn is on the left.

On the first floor of the brick house are two rooms of generous proportions (each approximately twenty feet square) with English-style fireplaces. Above are two rooms on the second floor and a garret on the third. On the east front, the brick is laid in English cross bond with alternating burnt and regular headers, creating quite a graphic pattern. The gable ends have parapets and finials and are finished along the top edge with "braiding" or "tumbling" in the brickwork. Perhaps elaborations of the original stoops, the two porches on the east front are later additions. They were in place by the mid-nineteenth century, if not before, as they are documented in a painting of that period by Richard Hubbard hanging in the house today.

The interconnecting parts of the Bronck house stand in a mature grove of oak trees, which adds greatly to the sense of antiquity of the place. At the rear of the house is a brick dependency of the late eighteenth or early nineteenth century, which was used as a kitchen. Approached across a small paved courtyard that links all the wings, it overlooks a pond, created in the 1950s by damming up the Coxsackie Creek to create a reservoir for museum fire protection.

The barns are wonderful examples of three different period styles. A late-eighteenth-century Dutch barn, dating from the era when this was a wheat farm, is closest to the house. Its original threshing floor, with three-inch-thick oak planks, is still in place. There is also an unusual thirteen-sided hay barn from 1835 and a large horsebarn, built about 1870. Like the house, these barns all contain the collections of the Greene County Historical Society, which owns and operates the site. Among the objects on view is a model, made in the 1960s on an immense scale, of the famous Catskill Mountain House, the huge Greek Revival hotel of 1824, the first celebrated resort hotel in the area, which stood above the Hudson just a few miles away.

That piece of historic Greene County architecture is lost, demolished as structurally unsound in 1963. But the buildings of the Bronck Museum are alive and beautifully curated today to teach us about changing lifestyle and taste in a single family who owned this farm over eight generations.

John DeWint House

Tappan, Rockland County, 1700

Two miles west of the Tappan Slote, the Dutch name for the Sparkill River where it flows into the Hudson, lies the village of Tappan.[1] According to Rosalie Fellows Bailey, the celebrated writer on Dutch houses, the lands in this part of New York, known as the Tappan Patent, were purchased from the Tappan Indians in 1681 and 1682 by a group of eight white men and three black African men from Bouwery Village on Manhattan Island, and five men from New Jersey. They were all farmers looking to make new homesteads for themselves, not real estate speculators or Lords of the Manor.[2]

Daniel DeKlerck (or DeClark), who became the leader of the original Tappan "Patentees," built this brick and stone house in 1700. DeKlerck emigrated from Holland to New Netherland in the 1670s. Thirty years later, he was a farmer with two hundred acres, a brewer, a leader in the community, and wealthy, as this house attests. 1700 is an early date for a two-room house with a center hall, built partly of brick laid in English bond and partly of dressed red sandstone brought from the high palisades lining the western edge of the Hudson.

In the 1740s, the house and farm were sold to John DeWint (1716–1795) of New York City, an early exemplar of the city gentleman wanting a country place. DeWint was a native of the West Indies, where he owned a sugar plantation.[3] As DeWint's guest, General Washington used the house, only twenty miles from West Point, as his headquarters four times between 1780 and 1783.

During his stay from August to October 1780, Washington foiled the treacherous plot of General Benedict Arnold to surrender the American garrison at West Point to the British, and Arnold's co-conspirator British Major John André was executed in Tappan while Washington was living here. Three years later, in May 1783, Washington entertained the British General Sir Guy Carleton. Their agenda was to plan the orderly evacuation of New York City by the British, and it was a festive occasion. Samuel Fraunces, New York City's top chef, came up to prepare the meal

The numerals 1-7-0-0 are worked into the brick on the west front.

OPPOSITE: *The main elevation is brick. The frame kitchen wing on the left is a modern reconstruction.*

from his own establishment in lower Manhattan, the still-famous Fraunces Tavern.[4]

The DeWint house originally fronted on a lane from the hamlet of Tappan, a few hundred feet away. Foot-high numerals—1700—are worked into the brick across the 49-foot length of the facade and fashioned of the dark, burnt headers of the brick. The central entrance is flanked by two large windows on either side. The gable ends are partially dressed red sandstone below and brick above, while the rear elevation is red sandstone, the brick having been reserved for the entrance facade.

The form and design are generally typical of the Dutch colonial houses of nearby northern New Jersey, although the use of load-bearing masonry walls rather than timber-framed construction is unusual at this early date. A particularly charming feature is the "spring eave," a slight kick or curving outward at the lower end of the steep roof. This element—also called "extended eaves" or a "Flemish overhang"—is often seen on Dutch vernacular houses of the lower Valley, but it does not appear in the north because of the heavier snow-loads there in the winter.

In plan, the house consists of a central hallway with exterior doors at both ends and a room measuring roughly 22 by 22 feet at each side. The rooms are handsome, with windows on the west and east, and fireplaces in the gable ends. Some original Dutch

The Delft tiles over the fireplace are original to the house. The cupboard holds a dinner service.

elements—"free-hanging" or jambless fireplaces, casement windows, an enclosed staircase—were replaced with English-style equivalents, probably in the early years of the DeWint ownership. The painted paneling and glazed cupboards of the fireplace walls are improvements of the mid-eighteenth century, but the fireplaces retain their original surrounds of Delft tiles illustrating Biblical stories. The garret was divided into bedchambers, perhaps after Washington's visits, as he is known to have occupied the main south room downstairs. The furnishings are of the mid to late 1700s.

Known as the "DeWint Mansion" in the eighteenth century, the house seems modest in comparison to the scale and ambition of the more imposing Bronck house upriver and the stylish Frederick Van Cortlandt house, built just across the Hudson in 1748. In materials and plan, the DeWint house anticipates the new Anglo-Dutch style of the mid-eighteenth century.

Surrounding the house is a garden distinguished for its venerable beech trees, spruces, and white pines. In recognition of Washington's membership in the fraternal order of the Masons, the house and garden have been restored and are maintained as a public museum by the Grand Lodge of Free and Accepted Masons of the State of New York.

CHAPTER 2

ANGLO-DUTCH HOUSES: THE COMING OF ENGLISH STYLE

A nineteenth-century woodcut of Van Cortlandt Manor.

The Dutch lost political control of New Netherland in 1664, but Dutch culture and architecture flourished right up until the period of the American Revolution. Especially in and around Albany, Dutch people and their traditions held sway long after the victory of the British. Nevertheless, Restoration England had needed the region for political and economic reasons, and after 1664, New York was an English colony. Dutchess County, on the east bank of the Hudson, was named not for the Dutch people, but for the Duchess of York, sister-in-law of Charles II. A new style of house design had developed in England from the period of the Restoration of the Monarchy in the seventeenth century through the first half of the eighteenth century, the early "Georgian" period of Kings George I and II. First felt in New York in the 1740s, the English Georgian influence soon changed the old Dutch house of the Hudson Valley.

Houses that combine elements of the Dutch vernacular tradition with English ideas are larger and richer than the earlier buildings, and they look entirely different. In the mid-eighteenth century, New York was economically very successful, and this affluence supported the development of a new type of New York house.

Only a handful of houses remains to illustrate the fusion of Dutch and English design ideas in the period before the War of Independence. The oldest is Philipse Manor Hall, expanded in the mid-1740s into perhaps the earliest extant two-story symmetrical five-bay house in the region, and the latest treated here is Wynkoop House, dating to 1772 but still firmly inside the Anglo-Dutch tradition.

What are the hallmarks of the new English domestic architecture, the so-called "Georgian" style, and from what tradition do they derive? First and most obviously, these are two- or two-and-a-half-story buildings, and their main identifying characteristic is the formal, symmetrical organization of the principal facade into five units, or bays. The central entrance bay on the first floor is flanked by pairs of twelve-over-twelve double-hung sash windows, with five windows on the second story lined up to correspond to those below. There are modest cornices with or without modillion blocks, and either hipped, gambrel, or hipped-gambrel roofs. Sometimes there is a classical balustrade at the eaveline or, on a hipped gambrel roof, at the break between the pitches.

The central entrance leads to a central hallway, extending through the main block of the building to the rear wall. There is usually an open staircase in this hall. Rooms of the same size and proportion flank the hall. There may be bedchambers upstairs rather than an open garret. These houses sometimes have plastered ceilings. Gone are smoky, jambless fireplaces, and fireplace walls are paneled and painted. By the 1750s, the influence of Rococo London is seen in carved chimneypieces, paneling, and plaster ceilings enriched with floral decorations.

As English as they may seem, most of these houses were built for Dutch families, and they may also retain many substantially Dutch characteristics, including joist and plank ceilings, enclosed staircases, thick vernacular turnings on balusters, divided doors, and brickwork around window openings in stone walls.

During this period, the names of designers, builders, and artisans first emerge. Still vernacular buildings, to be sure, Philipse Manor Hall and the Frederick Van Cortlandt house have carved woodwork attributed to the furniture maker Henry Hardcastle, and the John Ellison house is known to have been designed and built by a fascinating figure called William Bull.

Physical manifestations of a blending of Dutch and British culture unique to New York, this group of houses is one of the architectural wonders of America.

Van Cortlandt Manor House

Croton-on-Hudson, Westchester County, 1748

*Built by Pierre Van Cortlandt (1721–1814) at the
confluence of the Croton and Hudson Rivers, this
sandstone, granite, and brick house was the center of
the agricultural, milling, and shipping empire of the
most prosperous branch of the Van Cortlandt family.
A Dutch vernacular structure, perhaps dating from
the 1680s, now supports an early-eighteenth-century
addition. The Anglo-Dutch five-bay facade is visible
at the upper level of the porch, while the veranda itself
is probably a nineteenth-century design.*

The south facade was built in two phases and is not quite symmetrical.

Philipse Manor Hall

Yonkers, Westchester County, c. 1682–c. 1755

Philipse Manor Hall is one of the last remaining reminders of high-style English taste in pre-Revolutionary New York. This substantial manor was developed in stages by the three Frederick Philipses (I, II, and III) between about 1682 and 1755. The site overlooked the Neperhan River, later called the Saw Mill River, just a thousand feet or so uphill from the point where the Neperhan flowed into the Hudson. Originally, there were mills here because of the falls on the river, and both this early industrial site and the house were surrounded by a village and agricultural lands.

Frederick Philipse I (1626–1702) acquired the property from the heirs of Adriaen Van der Donck, a European-educated lawyer who had been granted 24,000 acres by the Dutch government in 1646. The birthplace and early life of Philipse are unrecorded, but by the early 1650s the young Dutchman was working as a carpenter-builder in New Amsterdam. He built a house for Peter Stuyvesant, and ultimately became a highly successful merchant, trader, and real estate speculator. In 1662, he married a daughter of the wealthy DeVries family (she came with a fleet of ships). In 1693, all of Frederick I's land holdings were granted a royal charter, and the Philipse Manor or Philipsborough was born. Philipse was considered the richest man in New York. His manor extended twenty-two miles north from Manhattan to the Croton River and from the Hudson five miles eastward to the Bronx River. The earliest part of Philipse Manor Hall, a Dutch vernacular structure built in the 1680s, is still visible in the western three bays of the south facade. It was probably a warehouse, since Frederick I lived in Manhattan.

The second Lord of the Manor was Frederick Philipse II (1695–1751), grandson of the first. By the 1720s, Frederick II must have transformed the warehouse into a residence because he was living at least part of the year on the estate. In the 1740s, he expanded the south facade by two bays into a five-bay elevation. His new south elevation is more or less, but not perfectly, symmetrical, and it represents an attempt to create an English-style house

This engraving reconstructs the high-style eighteenth-century garden in front of the east facade. After the building was converted to municipal use in 1868, a Civil War monument was erected on the lawn.

similar to those he would have seen during his student years in England between 1707 and 1716.[1] Under a hipped gambrel roof, the rectangular structure has a central entrance and large window openings, more or less symmetrically arranged and fitted with moveable twelve-over-twelve sash. Vestigial Dutch details include the divided door, a pent-roofed porch over a stone stoop, and the brick window surrounds. If, as it is now believed, this expansion dates to 1740–45, this is the oldest English Georgian-style house extant in New York State.

The third Lord of the Manor, Frederick Philipse III (1720–1786), created a grand family seat in the 1750s, adding on the east side a long wing made of brick, laid in Flemish bond. This elevation is eight bays long and two-and-one-half stories high, with two entrances. There is a classical balustrade on the hipped gambrel roof, and a modillion cornice at the roofline. An unusual element is the modillion cornice at the stringcourse with a pent roof over it. Here, now, is the rich Georgian statement, created by the thoroughly Anglophile great-grandson of the first Lord.

In this period, the house was enriched by terraced formal gardens on the east and north, and splendid interior architecture revealing an avid taste for English design and luxury. Two principal parlors, on the first and second floors, both on the southeast corner of the building, have elaborate carved decoration in the English Rococo style, newly arrived on American shores. The paneled walls include monumental carved chimneypieces, one with the head of a female deity and a broken scroll pediment, flanked by engaged, fluted, Ionic columns. The carving is attributed to the cabinetmaker Henry Hardcastle, known to have been working in New York City at the time.[2] The first-floor parlor has an elaborate Rococo ceiling with floral swags, birds, and two portrait heads, all created from molded papier maché. Other notable features from this period are the

New York Rococo carvings attributed to Henry Hardcastle enhance the east parlor. The ceiling ornament is executed in papier mâché

five-lobed fanlights over three exterior doors, and the mahogany staircase in the east hall.

The English colonial system had provided the context for the Philipse family's rise to wealth and power, and it is not surprising that Frederick III was a Loyalist in the Revolution. As a result, his estate was confiscated in 1779. He fled to New York City, and later to England, and the manor was sold by the American Commissioners of Forfeiture in 1785.

Throughout the next century, as Yonkers grew up around it, the Manor Hall was occupied by various private owners, until 1868, when it became the village hall. It was rather dramatically changed at this time by the addition of a great council chamber in the Gothic Revival style and the alteration of other rooms to serve municipal purposes. The important Georgian interiors were retained, and after a dangerous moment in the 1890s, when the building was very nearly ruined by municipal planners, it was miraculously saved by a generous benefaction from Eva Smith Cochran, heiress to a local carpet fortune. Her gift enabled New York State to purchase the site. After a major restoration in about 1911, the house was opened to the public as a museum, which it remains today.

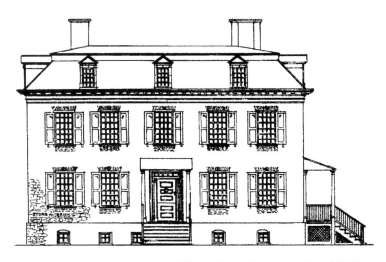

The south facade drawn by Donald Millar.

Frederick Van Cortlandt House

Van Cortlandt Park, The Bronx, 1748

As the crow flies, this handsome fieldstone house is about a mile and a half east of the Hudson, near the northern New York City limits. Not far away are the historic Woodlawn Cemetery (1863) and the New York Botanical Garden (1895).

Set deep within Van Cortlandt Park, originally the family's farm or "plantation," the house is surrounded by historic landscape and topographical features preserved in its parkland setting. The great house faces south across Tibbet's Brook, today swampy and shallow, but once an important source of waterpower on the estate and navigable to the Harlem River and thence to the Hudson. Nearby is Van Cortlandt Lake, created by damming the Brook for industrial purposes in 1699.

Approximately one hundred acres to the north of the house remain open—originally Van Cortlandt wheat fields and now playing fields known as the "Parade Ground." Across these fields, about a half-mile from the house, is a wooded knoll known to the Van Cortlandts as Vault Hill, a family burial site. To the southeast is a stretch of the old Albany Post Road, now a path roughly cobbled with shards of local stone, lined by ancient horse chestnut trees, and running parallel to the east front of the house.

Frederick Van Cortlandt (1699–1749), who built this house, was the grandson of the founder of the Van Cortlandt dynasty and a cousin of the family who lived at the immense Van Cortlandt Manor further north in Westchester. His mother was the stepdaughter of Frederick Philipse I, and thus the two great Dutch families of this area were closely related. Frederick grew up on

Manhattan Island near the family brewery, and it was his grandfather who began buying this land north of New York City in the seventeenth century.

The house is remarkable among New York houses of this date for its large size and sophistication. Constructed of a local gray stone known as "Fordham gneiss," the house stands two stories tall on a high foundation. The walls were once "parged" or "render coated" in a sandy-colored stucco to protect the stone and the cement pointing from the weather. On the front or south elevation, the house has a double hipped roof (with two pitches), and a symmetrical five-bay facade with a wide cornice and modillion blocks. Unique to the house are the small grotesque masks carved in the brownstone lintels above the windows. Following the extension of the south elevation at Philipse Manor by only a few years, this is the second New York house with a reliable date evincing the new English taste.

The house is L-shaped, which is probably its original configuration. Since the east facade is only slightly shorter than the south, the house appears nearly square from the southeast. The east front, originally facing the Albany Post Road, is not symmetrical, however, and the effect is much less imposing and less important than that achieved on the south. The east block has a gambrel roof and is, in this regard as well, less formal than the south.

The south-facing block of the house has a typical Georgian plan with two parlors flanking a squarish center hall. The east parlor is the grander of the two, with a carved mantel and overmantel attributed to Henry Hardcastle, the cabinetmaker to whom the Rococo carvings at Philipse Manor Hall are also attributed.[1] It makes sense that these two families would have known and retained the same New York City craftsman. In the west parlor, the raised paneling on the fireplace wall is original, complementing a restored eighteenth-century fireplace surrounded by blue and white tiles. The plan of the east block is similar, but the details are all less refined, suggesting this was where the business of the plantation was conducted.

The west parlor has a fine paneled fireplace wall and an important eighteenth-century kas painted in grisaille.

Given this house museum to operate in 1896 after the land was sold to the City, the National Society of Colonial Dames in the State of New York have performed a wonderful service in their stewardship and care. Donald Millar drew the house for his book *Measured Drawings of Some Colonial and Georgian Houses*, published in 1915. Just before World War I, apparently influenced by the craze for the Colonial Revival, the Dames commissioned the Rhode Island architect Norman Isham to improve and restore the building. His interventions, primarily new "Dutch" doors on the main east and south sides and new Georgian-style paneling in the east parlor and south hall, are of great interest today for those who study Colonial Revival taste. The distinguished architectural historian Abbott Lowell Cummings consulted to the Dames in the 1960s; his work included the restoration of the fireplace wall in the west parlor and the return to original condition of the interesting unfinished room on the third floor. All of this work only intensifies the eighteenth-century ambience of the house.

TOP: *Detail of mantel carving*

ABOVE AND OPPOSITE:
*The exceptionally fine carving
in the east parlor is attributed
to Henry Hardcastle.*

John Ellison House

Vail's Gate, Orange County, 1754

The Ellison house is a well-known landmark of the Revolutionary War. Located just down the road from the New Windsor Cantonment, where the Continental Army wintered in 1782, the house served as domicile and headquarters of General Henry Knox, George Washington's Chief of Artillery, and other officers during parts of the years 1779 to 1783. With their wives and aides-de-camp, these military men took over part of the house while the family continued to live there themselves. This circumstance is all the more remarkable because John Ellison (1736–1814) and his family, considered neutral in the Revolution, have always been suspected of secret Loyalist tendencies.

If the Ellisons wanted to have it both ways, so did the designer and builder of their house. William Bull (1689–1755) was an immigrant from Britain and a master mason, who had been building stone houses in the vicinity since the 1720s; this house, commissioned by John Ellison's father, Thomas, was Bull's last and best. Remarkably, a contract signed by Thomas Ellison and Bull in February of 1754 for a two-story stone house to be completed by that September survives and is exhibited in the house. It is unusual to know the identity of the builder or designer of a vernacular house of this early date, and even more so, to have the signed building contract.[1]

The Ellison house is a prime example of the stylistic blend of Anglo-Dutch. The southeast elevation is an English Georgian style, symmetrical, five-bay design, perhaps inspired by fashionable Manhattan houses of the period or perhaps by the south elevation of Philipse Manor Hall in Yonkers. In contrast, the rear facade is a totally asymmetrical design in the Dutch vernacular taste, very like the Jonathan Hasbrouck house in Newburgh of about 1724. This elevation features a long low roof, sweeping down almost to the ground to cover a lean-to, and only a few small windows.

Like the principal facades of both the Philipse and Van Cortlandt houses, the main elevation of the Ellison house

The rear façade (ABOVE) is Dutch vernacular, while the west end of the house (OPPOSITE) illustrates the marriage of English and Dutch vernacular style.

BELOW: *Plate 131 from Book VII of Serlio's treatise on house design reveals the Renaissance roots of the main facade design.*

illustrates English design exerting its influence on vernacular buildings in rural New York. In turn, it can be associated with the Classical houses of Italian Renaissance architects like Sebastiano Serlio. His designs, published in treatises, were brought to England by the architect Inigo Jones and developed throughout the 1600s and up until the mid-eighteenth century in English manor houses and country seats. It is interesting to compare the Ellison house with a plate from Serlio's treatise, *Five Books of Architecture*, published in English in 1611.[2]

British designs were promulgated by architectural handbooks first available in the colonies in the 1750s. Earlier technical guides for builders had not included designs for house elevations.[3] Bull may have consulted these new books, or he may have relied on his own training. Or he may responded to his client's direction. The affluent Ellison family—with a shipping business and their own wharves in Manhattan—had certainly seen very sophisticated new houses in the city, and perhaps had been to England.

But what about the vernacular rear facade of the house? In the 1750s, if the principal facade facing the main road was modern and elegant, the rear could be rather pokey and behind the fashion. The strategy of building houses with a fine and expensive

Fine paneling and plastered ceilings set the Ellison House apart from earlier New York houses.

Georgian facade in the front and an informal back facade with few or no windows was not unusual. In the Hudson Valley, it can be seen at Philipse Manor Hall, the Frederick Van Cortlandt house, the Wynkoop house, and even the Schuyler Mansion in Albany.

Inside, the house has a central hall with parlors to the left and right. The exposed joists and floorboards of traditional Dutch ceilings are still present, but there is an open stair rising in three runs and the fireplaces are English-style, with jambs. The fireplace walls in the four main rooms (two down, two up) are paneled. On the second floor, the Dutch garret has been replaced with finely finished rooms for sleeping.

Now sitting in a silent landscape, this house was formerly on the busy King's Highway. Just below the hill was the Ellison grist mill on Silver Stream, a tributary of Murderer's Creek, a tributary of the Hudson. The Ellison house is now operated as a museum by New York State. Our understanding of the evolution of architectural style in New York is greatly enhanced by this building, and its unassailable documentation as to date and design proves that it is a stylish link between the Dutch vernacular and Georgian styles.

Lithgow

Lithgow, Dutchess County, c. 1758–60

On a high and breezy hill looking out to the north and east, across the rolling hunt country of Millbrook, Lithgow sits politely and modestly as it has for almost 250 years. This was a sheep farm in the early years, as is attested to by eight-foot stone walls or sheep "fences" in the woods above the house. In the nineteenth century, it was a farm for fattening up cattle brought from western New York State by the Erie Canal and the Hudson and later became a dairy farm, like almost every old farm in rural New York State. Today Lithgow is home to fallow deer of an elegant English breed, peacocks, and screeching guinea fowl. The livestock may have changed over the centuries, but this has always been a gentleman's farm.

The land was originally part of the "Great Nine Partners' Patent." David Jamison, a Scottish Quaker, and his eight partners purchased a large section of northern Dutchess County in 1697, obtaining a Crown Patent for this massive real estate speculation, which included nine river lots on the east bank of the Hudson; the land was held in common among the original investors until 1734, when it was subdivided. It was around this period that many Quakers moved into Dutchess County from Westchester County and Connecticut.

When David Johnstone (1724–1809) inherited his grandfather Jamison's 734 acres, he and his wife and their ten children lived in New York City, where Johnstone was prominent in business and society. In the 1750s, he built this fine country house, naming it after Linlithgow in Scotland, his grandfather's birthplace. The record indicates that Johnstone retired early and moved up to the country permanently in the 1760s. Two hundred years later, in the 1960s, Lithgow's current owner, desiring a country seat and a place to create a major garden, also left New York City for the country, and, across two centuries, it is intriguing to compare the motives of these two men of affairs wishing to have quieter country lives.

This is a gambrel roof house of a remarkable type. Unlike almost all other gambrel roofs, which have two pitches, this roof

The south front (ABOVE) and the north front (OPPOSITE). The triple-pitch on the gambrel roof is very rare. The piazza on the north is a later addition.

The open stair rising to the garret is probably an alteration of the later eighteenth century. The house is furnished in Anglo-American country house taste.

has three. Although the main rooms are very large and high, the house appears to sit low—a story and a half. The overall line of the roof is low, creating an elegant profile, sweeping downward from two massive chimneys. At the time Lithgow was built, gambrels were often used on large houses such as this—two rooms deep and therefore requiring a larger span from front to back.

Although the house was much altered and improved in the later eighteenth century to make it more Georgian in feeling, various aspects of the building still reveal Dutch influence, including the shed dormers and the divided Dutch doors at the principal south and north entrances. The house is of post and beam construction, with brick infill in the walls, a rather late indication of Dutch construction. The infill rises to the roof in the gable ends, and is also used in interior walls. It is invisible on the exterior of the house, which is sheathed in wide weatherboarding with a beaded edge.

The floor plan features a spacious center hall divided into two parts—the larger "front" hall on the north side, and the smaller on the south. The open stair is in a side hall. Helen Wilkinson Reynolds, author of two important books on Hudson Valley houses, writes that the original stair was probably enclosed, as in Dutch houses, and the current, open stair is perhaps from the late eighteenth century.[1] Other post-Revolutionary alterations include the fireplace walls in the two main (north) parlors, which Reynolds believes were probably originally paneled in the Georgian fashion of 1760, the paneling having been removed perhaps in the 1790s. Along the way, the second floor, which may have been an open garret space originally, was partitioned into bedrooms, perhaps after the Revolutionary War.

The main floor rooms have 12-foot ceilings and large proportions, and there is a basement under the original section with many rooms for storage and slave quarters. According to the current owner, thirty slaves were kept by the Johnstones and recorded in the census of 1790. Slave holding was common in New York at this period; in 1749, 15 percent of the population of New York were African slaves.[2]

The Johnstone family had died out by the early 1800s, and the house came into the Smith-Wheaton family, which owned it until the days of the present owner. The Smiths are believed to have added the rectangular sidelights and transoms around the main north and south doors and the expansive veranda on the north facade, probably around 1814.

There is a local legend that the Smith family introduced black locust trees *(Robinia pseudocacia)* to Dutchess County, bringing these trees from Long Island around 1814. They are said to be the parent trees from which all of the many black locusts of the Hudson River Valley are descended. Although these may not have been the first black locusts in this area—various earlier houses claim to have older trees—it is plausible that they were imported. Botanical scientists tell us that black locust was not native to American soil this far north; it was more likely to have been found in the wild in places further south, in Pennsylvania or Virginia, or perhaps even Long Island. As black locust is now fully naturalized in the central Hudson Valley, it is surprising to think of it as an invasive species.[3]

Around 1910, the Wheatons added a major new service wing to the east end of the house, in the style of the original gambrel roofed structure. Now part of that addition has been pulled down, but other elements remain from this period— some interior details in the old house, and a handsome brick and stucco garage.

The garden laid out over the past forty years by the current gentleman farmer includes two well-placed lakes and a Greek Revival temple, or "eye-catcher," at the top of a hill far away, but on axis with the center hall of the house. There are formal and informal gardens, a rockery, a double allée of lime trees *(tilia cordata)*, and a vast deer park stretching across a canted-up hillside above one of the lakes. Thus, the old house has been provided with an expansive landscape setting in the Anglo-American taste. David Johnstone, the first gentleman farmer on this land, would be well pleased.

Wynkoop House

Stone Ridge, Ulster County, c. 1767–72

With the presence of a manor house, the Wynkoop house presides over the main street of the lovely old village of Stone Ridge. The road west from Kingston is lined with eighteenth-century limestone houses, but none on the scale of Wynkoop. The oldest of these houses are story-and-a-half Dutch vernacular buildings, and, like the Wynkoop house, they are all built of warm tan-gray Onondaga limestone, the "stone" of Stone Ridge and Marbletown, the surrounding township. These Dutch houses were built on this road because it was an important early highway in and out of the old city of Kingston, the capital of New York from 1777 to 1797 and an important river port since the seventeenth century. Some Dutch families, including the Wynkoops, had major shipping businesses in Kingston, and even traded with the West Indies.

"Stoney Ridge," as it was called then because of the limestone outcrops flanking the highway, was suburban, in a sense, to Kingston, although it was above all a farming settlement. For generations, the Wynkoop house has been widely recognized as the principal house of the hamlet. This was already true when General George Washington spent the night of November 15, 1782, in the southwest bed chamber, and it is true today, when the house has been magnificently preserved and conserved as a work of art by its current owners, an architect and an art historian.

This building is a fine and elegant example of the Anglo-Dutch style. In the middle of the eighteenth century, Hudson River society achieved considerable prosperity, and the Wynkoops were members of the wealthy Dutch merchant and trading class. Later to play significant roles in the Revolutionary War and as a civic leader, Cornelius Wynkoop (1746–1795)

*The dining room was originally the main parlor. All of the painted
surfaces in this room are thought to be eighteenth century.*

bought his farm here on this ridge in 1766, and built this tall and
prepossessing house soon after. He and his builders were well
acquainted with Dutch vernacular building traditions, and there
are many elements associated with early houses—the rough limestone masonry on the rear and side facades; divided exterior
doors; chunky turnings on the "gum wood" balusters of the open
staircase; and the ceilings in the downstairs hall and upstairs
rooms constructed with unpainted, beaded-edged floor joists
and exposed floorboards.

But in 1767, there were many New York examples of houses in
the English taste. Wynkoop obviously wanted a larger house than
those of his neighbors and he desired something less Dutch. He
built a symmetrical, five-bay, two-and-one-half story structure measuring 60 feet across and 40 feet high. He covered it with the two-
pitch gambrel roof spanning the deep floor plan he wanted—a
central hall with an open stair, and two rooms on either side. He
plastered the ceilings in his main chambers on the first floor and
installed handsome Georgian paneled fireplace walls around his

English fireplaces in the principal rooms downstairs and two of the
bedchambers upstairs. Several of these are surrounded by fine
Delft tiles in blue and white and in manganese and white. His
splendid staircase is a robust piece of casework, rising in four wide
runs from the first floor to the high garret, or third floor. At the
top, it is open to the garret above. His many, large windows clearly
demonstrate his interest in the new Anglo-American taste. What
Wynkoop had created was a new Georgian vernacular house with
many Dutch elements—a blending of the two styles.

All of the beautifully crafted moveable window sash are pow-
ered by very rare, original counterweight systems. Both the lower
and the upper sash are moveable.[1] Most retain their original eighteenth-century crown glass as well as their original paneled exterior
shutters and shutter hardware. The current owners believe the windows may have been made in New York City and shipped up-river.[2]

The interiors of the house are almost perfectly preserved and
are notable for their antique (many eighteenth-century) painted
surfaces—a rich green on two paneled fireplace walls and

The center hall has a Dutch vernacular ceiling of joists and floorboards, but the ceiling in the parlor (to the right) is plastered.

OPPOSITE: *The bedchambers are in original condition.*

whitewash on the plaster. Amazingly, the wide white pine floorboards retain their original hand-planed and unfinished surfaces.

The foundations are local bluestone, with limestone walls above. The limestone of the front facade is partially dressed above the water table, but on the sides and back the masonry is rougher, some of it almost rubble. On the main facade, the stones are laid in a graduated pattern with the largest toward the bottom, and there is no sign that the wall was ever parged or covered with stucco. There is a wide, white-painted cornice with eighteenth-century modillion blocks. A box gutter, added about 1840, projects beyond the cornice.

The property has many elements of historical significance. In front of the house is a venerable, perhaps two-hundred-year-old, line of black locust trees planted at ten-foot intervals, just back from the road. To the south is a long, rectangular wagon shed (c. 1767), and a recently installed eighteenth-century Dutch barn, moved from Otsego County, New York, to the site of an original structure, long ago collapsed. The tall picket fence

surrounding the front lawn is a reconstruction of a c. 1818 fence based on a pale, or picket, found inside the house and an old photograph. The kitchen at the south end and behind the main house is an earlier Dutch house built about 1719. It is believed that the large new house of Cornelius Wynkoop was grafted onto the earlier structure.[3]

When the Wynkoops sold the property in 1818, it went to the Lounsbery family, which included several New York State political leaders. The last member of that family, Sarah Lounsbery, was born here in 1891. When she died in 1988, the house still had no bathroom, and there was electricity in only two rooms. The only alterations to the structure over the centuries have been certain interior changes made to one downstairs parlor about 1840; the addition of the box gutter at the same date; the front porch about 1870; the alteration of the second story and other aspects of the kitchen in the 1930s; and a few restorations to windows and chimneys made in the 1990s.

CHAPTER 3

AMERICAN GEORGIAN STYLE

In the mid-1700s, British ideas about domestic architecture gradually began to overwhelm Dutch elements of design. Once somewhat provincial, New York began to catch up with Boston, Philadelphia, and Virginia in its sophistication about English house design. The elements that first appeared in Anglo-Dutch houses had taken firm hold by about 1760, when the Schuyler Mansion was built in Albany. That house retains no vestiges of Dutch style, although it was built as the seat of one of the great patrician Dutch families of New York. Schuyler would become a distinguished American Revolutionary leader, but he lived in the style of a British aristocrat. Many American Georgian houses of this period were built in the English taste by men who became Patriot leaders.

The term "Georgian" is used here to describe the later-eighteenth-century New York houses that threw off all Dutch features and embraced English domestic design concepts. In Britain, "Georgian" is a broad rubric, encompassing multiple styles that emerged during the reigns of Kings George I, II, III, and IV—the Baroque style of Christopher Wren, the Palladianism of William Kent, the Classicism of James Gibbs, the Neoclassicism of Robert Adam at the end of the century, and the Regency style of the early 1800s.

Less confusingly, American Georgian houses emulate middle-sized English houses rather than the Palladian mansions and stately homes of the period. These more modest buildings were modeled on the seventeenth-century, Renaissance-inspired designs of Inigo Jones, and they proliferated in the English countryside between 1700 and 1750.

In America, these houses are usually two- or two-and-a-half story rectangular blocks with a five or seven-bay front and a hipped or gambrel roof. Like their peers in Virginia and Maryland, the New York houses are often brick. Symmetrical plans are based on a center hall with two rooms, chamber and antechamber, on either side and an open, decoratively carved staircase. Fireplace walls in the main rooms are often articulated with paneled chimneypieces flanked by paneled doors or cupboards.

New York had profited enormously from supplying the British army during the French and Indian War, and these new houses were built for sophisticated, affluent families with business and friends in New York City and London. The Enlightenment was at hand—but so was the Revolution.

Henry I. Van Rensselaer House
Greenport, Columbia County, 1785

After his service as an officer in the Revolutionary War, Henry I. Van Rensselaer built this formal brick house near Claverack, south of the immense Van Rensselaer Manor. Possibly inspired by the pre-War Schuyler Mansion in Albany, the house incorporates features found on several other New York Georgian houses, in particular the short Palladian or Venetian window over the front door. The triple-hung windows are later alterations of the Federal period. The pediment over the door surround is modern.

Rendering by the Albany architect Philip Hooker showing the six-sided vestibule added to the main facade during the Federal period.

The New-York Historical Society

Schuyler Mansion

Albany, Albany County, 1761

This rosy red brick Georgian mansion might be called an American "powerhouse," in the sense that it was clearly designed and built as the seat of power for a rich and influential family. For forty years, Philip Schuyler (1733–1804) and his wife, the very rich Catherine Van Rensselaer, used this beautiful house to entertain a distinguished stream of visitors, including George Washington, Benjamin Franklin, and many Frenchmen, among them the Marquis de Lafayette, the Marquis de Chastellux, and the Vicomte de Noailles. Their daughter, Elizabeth, married Alexander Hamilton in the main drawing room in 1780.

The Schuylers lived at the pinnacle of Colonial society. Philip was descended from Philip Pieterson Schuyler, one of two sons of an Amsterdam baker who came to the Hudson Valley to make their fortunes. His children married into the most established Albany Dutch families, and his son Pieter Schuyler became the city's first mayor, remembered today for taking four distinguished Iroquois to London in 1710 to meet Queen Anne. Philip Schuyler, great-grandson of the founder, achieved success in political, military, and business affairs. He owned real estate and lumber mills and traded in timber, grain, flax, and hemp. After serving with distinction in the French and Indian and Revolutionary Wars, he was active in New York State politics as a State Senator and a gubernatorial candidate. Such a rich and public figure naturally wanted a great and stylish house.

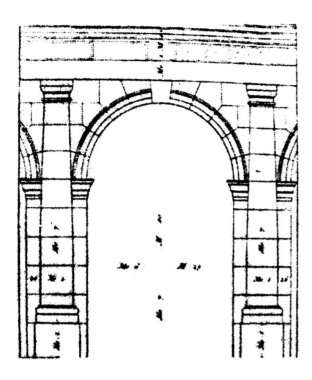

An illustration from William Halfpenny's builder's guide shows the likely precedent for the archway in the wall between front and back halls.

Construction began in 1761, while Schuyler was in England conducting business for his friend John Bradstreet, a quartermaster in the English army, who stayed in Albany and acted as general contractor for the house.

Schuyler first saw his house from the Hudson as he sailed towards Albany on his return from London in 1762. Sited on a hill above the grazing pastures owned by the Dutch church just south of the Albany stockade, it must have been an astonishing vision from the river. Measuring 63 feet in length, the house stands on a high foundation, its two tall main stories covered by a double-hipped roof with a Chinese Chippendale balustrade. The cluster of three windows in the center of the second floor, corresponding to the central door and flanking hall windows below, is a feature found in English houses of the eighteenth century. The brickwork is English cross bond, making a distinct diamond pattern, with jack arches serving as lintels over the many windows. In contrast, the rear elevation is an asymmetrical, utilitarian design with few windows. The stylish Georgian design and almost all of the very large windows were reserved for the "public" sides of the house—the east front and the north and south ends.

The interior was luxurious and elegantly fitted-out. Bradstreet commissioned work from master craftsmen, who are all known by name today. John Gaborial, a Boston woodworker who is thought to have created the staircase and the paneled fireplace walls, may

Flocked wallpapers in bright colors were favored by Philip Schuyler.

OPPOSITE: *The vestibule added in the Federal period is attributed to Philip Hooker.*

also have turned the elaborate balusters of the stair rail. The design, incorporating three different spiral turnings on each step, is a fashionable New England detail. Separating the formal entrance from the rear stair hall is a "screen wall" with an arched opening flanked by pilasters. This design, very similar to one at Carter's Grove, the great Virginia plantation house of about 1749, derives from the architectural handbook of William Halfpenny, published in many editions in London in the 1740s and 1750s and known to have been in Schuyler's library around 1790.

During his London visit, Schuyler made many luxurious purchases for the house, including a vast quantity of crown glass for the windows and wallpapers, both extravagant hand-painted scenes and brilliantly colored flocked patterns, then in vogue in England.[1] Schuyler worked at finishing the house throughout the 1760s—there are records of a 1767 delivery of marble fireplace surrounds from a Philadelphia dealer, for example—and the finishing touches were all in the high-style English Georgian taste.

The house was known for its sophisticated gardens—the famous 1794 plan of Albany by Simeon DeWitt detailed the layout of the Schuyler garden. A formal drive swept uphill to the front of the house around the sloping lawn. To the south was a formal parterre, probably for flowers, and there were orchards to the north. Schuyler was an agriculturist and fruit-grower famous for

breeding the Schuyler gage plum, prized in New York State for many generations.

After Scuyler's death in 1804, his property was divided among his children. The house passed out of the family by 1806 and went through several hands until it was bought by John Bryan, who made changes in the newly fashionable Federal taste. In addition to painting the brick and installing large pane six-over-six window sash, he added the eccentric but beautiful six-sided vestibule attributed to the Albany architect Philip Hooker (1766–1837). An 1818 watercolor by Hooker in the New-York Historical Society illustrates the house in its Federal guise.

Throughout the nineteenth century, the house had multiple owners and was at one point converted to a Catholic orphanage. Since 1917, the house has been a museum owned and operated by the State of New York, and interpreted to the time of Philip Schuyler. The windows are currently fitted with twelve-over-twelve moveable sash, which reproduce the design thought to be original.[2] Flocked and scenic wallpapers, similar to those Schuyler bought, are being reinstalled today. The hemlock floors have been scrubbed and left bare, and the large, square rooms contain much good mid- and late-eighteenth century American and English furniture. There is no better house in New York to visit for a comprehensive look at sophisticated Anglo-American taste in the period of the Revolution.

The upstairs hall has French scenic wallpaper that was installed in the 1800s. It may soon be replaced. The elaborate balusters are attributed to John Gaborial, a New England craftsman.

PAGES 75–76: *This is the bedroom where the British General John Burgoyne was housed after his surrender at Saratoga. The paneling of the fireplace wall is bold and notable.*

LEFT: *Clermont is a palimpsest of styles from Georgian through Second Empire to Colonial Revival.*

Clermont

Germantown, Columbia County, c. 1750; Rebuilt 1778–81

C lermont is the earliest of the grand riverfront estates in the Hudson River Valley. The original house was built by Robert Livingston Jr. in about 1750, on a bluff overlooking the river. In its survival through dramatic events and as the seat of the great and distinguished Livingston family, Clermont has been celebrated from the beginning as one of the finest Hudson River manor houses. "Livingston Valley," as the Hudson River Valley is sometimes called, is not inappropriate because there is an unbroken history of Livingston ownership, residence, and hegemony in Dutchess and Columbia counties, in Albany, and New York City, from 1686 to the present day.

The line began in the New World with Robert Livingston (1654–1728), who fled from Scotland to the Netherlands because of religious persecution under Charles II. In the Netherlands, he learned Dutch, which was useful indeed when he arrived at Albany (or "Fort George" as the British first named it) in 1672. Six years later, he married the patrician Alida Schuyler Van Rensselaer and went on to prosper in Anglo-Dutch society. In 1686, he received a Crown grant from King James II for Livingston Manor, 160,000 acres stretching from the Hudson River to what is today the western boundary of Massachusetts, including ten miles of riverfront. Livingston had already purchased smaller acreages from the local Indians on the eastern and western edges of the manor as it was to be. It has never been entirely clear how he came to own all the

The west front has one of the greatest views across the river to the Catskill Mountains.

land that stretched between, but the British government always supported his claim to the whole manor, and it was confirmed by Governor Robert Hunter in 1715.[1]

Clermont, originally a 13,000-acre estate at the extreme southwest corner of the manor, was Robert Livingston's bequest to his son Robert Livingston Jr. (1688–1775), a reward, it is said, for the younger Livingston's apprehension of an Indian intruder in an earlier family house. With the house Robert Livingston Jr. built at Clermont in about 1750, the history of the "Clermont Livingstons" begins. Robert Livingston Jr. was succeeded there by his son Judge Robert R. Livingston (1718–1775) and his wife, Margaret Beekman Livingston (1724–1800), the daughter of a wealthy Dutchess County family, much respected for her fine mind and good judgment. Their son was the highly distinguished Chancellor Robert R. Livingston Jr. (1746–1813), who held the state's highest judicial office. This Livingston played a prominent role in the young nation, helping to draft the Declaration of Independence, administering the oath of office to George Washington, and serving Thomas Jefferson as Minister to France in Paris, where he negotiated the Louisiana Purchase in 1803. In Paris, Chancellor

Livingston met the inventor Robert Fulton and later became a partner on his steamboat project. The first steamboat journey was staged from New York to Albany in 1807, and the boat, now known as the Clermont, stopped to greet the Livingstons at the Clermont landing.

The longevity of Clermont Manor is owed in no small measure to the courage and tenacity of Margaret Beekman Livingston during and after the dire events of 1777. With Kingston in flames, the British, led by Sir John Vaughn, came across the river to burn Clermont, as the Livingstons were well-known Patriots. Forewarned of the attack, Margaret was able to flee with some possessions. She soon returned, and by 1778 was engaged in rebuilding. The Georgian house she re-established—a four-square, rectangular house, with a symmetrical facade of five bays, a low-pitched roof, and a roof balustrade—is known to us through a drawing by Alexander Robertson in the New-York Historical Society.

Today, Clermont is quite changed, with wings at the north and south ends (1814 and 1831) and the addition of a third story covered by a steep slate mansard roof in 1874. Alterations to the 1778 riverfront elevation include the Colonial Revival front door and surrounding windows and the quaint shutters, all "improvements" of the 1920s. The interiors of the center block are intact, except for Federal architraves on the doors and mantelpieces thought to be from around 1800. The elegant French crystal chandelier, c. 1805, in the front drawing room and other Neoclassical elements may have been added between 1800 and 1805 by Francophile

A portrait of the distinguished Margaret Beekman Livingston by John Wollaston, c. 1749–52, hangs in Clermont today.

OPPOSITE:
The Georgian stair hall is divided into two parts by the high arch.

family members.[2] Today, the wings house the kitchen and a Victorian library of 1893.

What has never changed is the unsurpassed view of the Catskill Mountains. From the front door of the house, straight to the west, "the entire eastern wall of the Catskills . . . may be grasped in one delighted glance."[3] This view includes the half million acres west of the river once owned by the Livingstons of Clermont.

Several important early landscape features survive, including a lilac walk created in the 1830s and the eighteenth-century wagon road, which winds in romantically from the public road, traveling through venerable allées of white pine and black locust. The gardens include a flower garden known to have been designed by Alice Delafield Clarkson Livingston in 1908. The formal garden of lawn and trees directly behind the house dates from the 1920s.

In 1962, when the seventh generation of Livingstons moved out, Clermont was given to New York State, and it is now open to the public. The last daughter of that generation, Honoria Livingston McVitty, lived nearby until her death in 2000. A number of her Livingston cousins still live in important houses on the river.

CHAPTER 4

HOUSES OF THE NEW REPUBLIC: THE FEDERAL NEOCLASSICAL STYLES

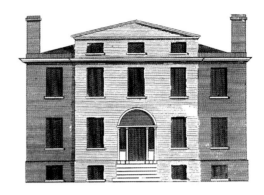

The Federal Neoclassical styles emerged around the time of the Treaty of Paris in 1783. New York had suffered terribly in the War of Independence, but a period of tremendous economic expansion followed, leading up to the opening of the Erie Canal in 1825. In trade, commerce, banking, real estate speculation, and population growth, New York City was becoming the first city of the new nation. This unprecedented prosperity spawned a period of wildly active house building in the Hudson Valley. Some builders were landed gentry desiring new manor houses. Others were upper-middle-class people who had prospered in the War or families newly grown rich in expanding industrial towns like Troy. A few wanted county villas for summer entertaining and respite from town life.

Just as pre-Revolutionary American houses were provincial versions of earlier English Georgian buildings, the new Federal style was for the most part a conservative, even puritanical, version of the Neoclassical style that had been developed and promulgated in England by the architect Robert Adam. The "Adam style" was derived from Adam's archeological research in Rome, beginning in the 1750s. After 1773, when Adam and his brother James published the first volume of their influential treatise, *The Works in Architecture*, the Neoclassical house became the new fashion in England and later in America.

The exteriors of American Neoclassical houses were often very plain—two- or three-story rectangular masses, often built of brick with stone details, with flat surfaces and shallow roof profiles. Inside there was a new freedom in planning and new technology in carpentry. Behind a chaste front might be curving and cantilevered stairs and elaborately carved wood and plaster ornament based on ancient Roman and Italian Renaissance designs.

The Federal style quickly became fashionable, especially in New England. Sophisticated patrons wanted English-style houses, just as they had before the Revolution, but in the new taste. Charles Bulfinch of Boston and Samuel McIntire of Salem, Massachusetts, specialized in this style, and many Federal period houses in the Hudson River Valley followed their lead.

A second strong influence on New York Neoclassicism came from France. This significant aspect of Hudson Valley Federal architecture is distinct from the Adamesque style. With Thomas Jefferson, various Hudson River grandees, including the Livingstons, adopted a French-inspired Federal style, which also drew on Italian Renaissance and ancient Roman precedents, but was far less conservative than the New England interpretation.

In these houses, free and unusual floor plans, absence of center halls, sets of octagonal, oval, or semi-circular rooms, and a general interest in geometrical abstraction, reveal the influence of late-eighteenth-century French Neoclassicism. Some may even have been designed by French architects working in New York in the 1790s and afterward.

Positioned between New England and the southern states, and between aristocratic Federalism and democratic Jeffersonian thinking, the Hudson River Valley encompasses Federal period houses in a wide range of styles that exhibit many new architectural ideas deriving from both British and French design. Perhaps nowhere else in America are such varied examples of Federal Neoclassicism to be enjoyed.

Locust Lawn
Gardiner, Ulster County, c. 1814

This frame house was built for Josiah Hasbrouck (1755–1821), whose family was prominent among the original group of French Huguenot settlers who came to the New Paltz area in 1677. It is thought that Locust Lawn was designed directly from Plate 55 (ABOVE) in Asher Benjamin's The American Builder's Companion: Or A System of Architecture Particularly Adapted to the Present Style of Building, *first published in 1806. The massing evokes an Italian villa with its central element rising to create a third floor, while the matched-board siding gives the house the feel of a masonry structure. Currently under restoration, the house retains its original collection of fine early-nineteenth-century furniture and decorative arts.*

A drawing by Douglas Bucher recreates the original design of the house. The west front was altered by the addition of the Greek Revival porch.

Ten Broeck Mansion

Albany, Albany County, 1798

Known as Prospect and later as Arbour Hill, this imposing Federal mansion was built by the Revolutionary War hero General Abraham Ten Broeck (1734–1810). Ten Broeck was a fifth generation American of Dutch descent and an imposing figure in the society and public affairs of late-eighteenth-century Albany. Following in the footsteps of his father, who had been mayor of Albany as well as Commissioner of Indian Affairs, Abraham Ten Broeck served as mayor twice, once in the late 1770s, and again twenty years later. He was a delegate to the Second Continental Congress in Philadelphia in 1775, and was made a general the following year. In 1777, with General Horatio Gates, he was victorious at the decisive battles of Saratoga and Bemis Heights that ensured American control of the Hudson. His later civic interests included serving as first president of the Albany Public Library and helping to establish Union College.

General Ten Broeck and his wife, Elizabeth Van Rensselaer, lived most of their adult lives in the center of Albany in a modest Dutch-style house. The great fire of 1797 burned them out, along with a large section of the old city. Even though they were both 63 years of age at the time, they decided to build a new house in the country, north of Albany proper, on property that had been granted to Ten Broeck some years earlier, in a feudal, perpetual

The cantilevered stair rises to the third floor.

OPPOSITE: *All the interiors were remodeled in the Greek Revival style.*

Walter Launt Palmer,
Library at Arbour
Hill, *1878. Today the
Victorian interiors have
been returned to the
Greek Revival style.*

*Albany Institute
of History & Art*

lease-hold arrangement, by the Patroon Stephen Van Rensselaer. The house would face east from a hill overlooking the Hudson and the old Van Rensselaer Manor—a view that after 1825 would include the mouth of the Erie Canal.

The Ten Broeck Mansion was one of the four great Albany houses. The others were the Schuyler Mansion (1761), the Van Rensselaer Manor (1765), and Cherry Hill (1767), also a Van Rensselaer house. All but the Manor are still extant, a testament to the long prominence of the families who built them.

The Ten Broeck Mansion recalls the fine, freestanding brick houses that Charles Bulfinch designed for his sophisticated clients

in Boston between 1790 and 1805. The architectural historians Walter Richard Wheeler and Douglas Bucher attribute the Ten Broek house to the Albany architect Philip Hooker on the basis of its design, which was advanced for Albany in this period. The two-story east facade is a classic essay in the American Federal style, with five bays, a central entrance, and six-over-six double-hung sash. Under the shallow pitch of the gable is a modest eaves cornice; a roof balustrade joins the brick parapets below the chimneys at the gable ends. Executed in brick with brownstone trim, the facades are flat and plain, without quoining or rustication. This Federal characteristic again evokes Boston and Bulfinch—

The back parlor has a Classical secretary-bookcase by the important Albany furniture maker John Meads (1777–1859).

perhaps the first Harrison Gray Otis house of 1795–96. The house was originally painted a light color, perhaps gray.

The generally accepted construction date of 1798 is early for some of the advanced Federal elements to appear in an Albany house. According to Douglas Bucher, the "geometrical" or cantilevered spiral staircase is probably the first such staircase built in Albany. Bulfinch incorporated similar stairs in his houses around 1800; illustrations of this form appeared as early as 1792 in a Boston edition of *Practical Builder*, an architectural handbook by the English architect William Pain.[1] Pain's handbooks and those of other British architects appearing in the 1780s and 1790s were all for sale in New York and Boston by the time the Ten Broeck house went up in 1798.

The Greek Revival porches, Ionic on the front, Doric on the rear, were added by a subsequent owner, perhaps the King family, who lived in the house between about 1837 and 1842. Most of the interior architectural elements—mantelpieces, door and window architraves, and the pairs of Ionic columns flanking sliding doors—are of the Greek Revival period as are the sidelights and square transom of the main door, which together form a window wall facing the river.

In the later nineteenth century, the Olcotts, an important Albany banking family, owned the house. Two paintings by the wonderful Albany artist Walter Launt Palmer, both now at the Albany Institute of History and Art, document the Victorian interiors and furnishings of the Olcott occupancy.

The east front as redesigned
by Alexander Jackson Davis.

Montgomery Place

Annandale-on-Hudson, Dutchess County, 1804–5

Of all the wonderful houses the Livingston family built on the Hudson, Montgomery Place is perhaps the richest in history. There are few American houses more patrician, with a more patriotic history, or more revealing of American taste as it changed throughout the nineteenth century. Few house museums better illustrate the many layers of style that rest upon one another in a house that descended through generations of one family for two hundred years.

Montgomery Place is much more than a house museum, however. It is a 434-acre estate, an intact historic landscape with a strong connection to mid-nineteenth century landscape history and to Andrew Jackson Downing (1815–1852), the famous horticulturist, nurseryman, and landscape and architectural theorist. The estate is adjacent to the charming hamlet of Annandale-on-Hudson, with its store of vernacular Federal and Greek Revival cottages. But the most interesting aspect of Montgomery Place is the architecture of the house itself. There have been two phases of architecture here: the original Federal design of the early years of the nineteenth century, and the two mid-century redesigns by the prominent architect Alexander Jackson Davis (1803–1892).

Château de Montgomery, as Montgomery Place was first called, was built by Janet Livingston Montgomery (1743–1828), the widow of General Richard Montgomery, who was killed during the Battle of Quebec in 1775. After her husband's death, Janet stayed on in their house in Dutchess County until 1802. At the age of 59, she bought this working farm on the river and in 1804–5

The riverfront or west elevation.

OPPOSITE: *The pavilion by
Alexander Jackson Davis.*

built a new house. In this, she followed the example of her mother, Margaret Beekman Livingston, who had rebuilt Clermont, just a few miles up the river, in 1778, during her own widowhood and whose ten surviving children and their descendants built some thirty-six houses on the river between 1790 and 1940.[1]

The historian Roger Kennedy writes that Janet asked her brother Chancellor Robert Livingston, then Jefferson's Minister to France, for mail-order house plans from Paris for her new house.[2] In spite of this request, which may never have been answered, and in spite of the term "château," there is nothing very clearly French about the Federal design for Montgomery Place. It is an interesting theory, however, as the Livingstons were Francophiles, and in some of their houses (Arryl House, built by the Chancellor at Clermont, for example) they preferred the new French-inspired Federal architecture to more conservative, London-inspired designs.

Like several other Federal-period houses nearby, notably Edgewater and the Jacob Rutsen Van Rensselaer house, Montgomery Place has a pair of elegant drawing rooms. Here they comprise the whole riverfront elevation. Each room has three long windows extending to the floor on its river side, creating a six-bay elevation with no central entrance or hall. The east facade, which looks out over acres of rolling lawn with mature specimen trees, is more conventional, consisting of five bays with a central entrance.

The library is furnished with objects owned by generations of Livingstons and Delafields.

OPPOSITE: *In the hallway are portraits of President Andrew Jackson, under whom Edward Livingston (1764–1836) served as Secretary of State and Minister to France.*

The rectangular massing of the original Federal house with its shallow, hipped roof is still visible, but there is a wealth of later, romantic additions: three major Classical Revival porches, balustraded terraces, urns used as finials, and a general frosting layer of classically inspired details applied to the sand-finished stucco of the building. These elements are the mid-century improvements of Alexander Jackson Davis, the important New York architect of the Romantic Revival styles—Greek, Gothic, and Classical.

Janet Montgomery bequeathed the Château to her brother Edward Livingston, Mayor of New York and Minister to France under President Jackson, who, in turn, left the house to his wife,

Louise. In 1841, she commissioned Davis to add the south wing and the open pavilion on the north side. The pavilion, with its high arcade, articulated by engaged Corinthian columns and framing wide views of the river, is unique in American architecture. Later, in 1863, Davis was engaged again, this time by Coralie Livingston Barton, who had inherited the house from her mother, to add the grand semi-circular portico on the east front, the terraces and balustrade, and the west terrace. When Davis and Mrs. Barton corresponded in 1863, they referred to the Temple of Vesta, in Tivoli, just outside Rome, as the model for the extravagant portico.[3] The Livingston-Barton family may have seen the

The dining room (ABOVE) and the yellow drawing room (OPPOSITE) extend the full length of the riverfront of the house.

Temple of Vesta. Well-travelled Americans of the period would have visited Rome and perhaps journeyed out to Tivoli to see the ancient sites.[4]

With these additions and encrustations, Montgomery Place became the showplace of the Hudson. Its horticultural distinction added to its renown. Janet Montgomery had once operated commercial gardens, a fruit farm, and a nursery. Edward Livingston enthusiastically developed the landscape in the 1830s. The English architect Frederick Catherwood built a major conservatory (now gone) in 1838 before Andrew Jackson Downing became involved in the late 1840s. The Livingston and Barton family members who developed the arboretum at Montgomery Place were avid plant collectors; Downing sold plants to them and helped design some of the flowerbeds. In his 1847 article, "A Visit to Montgomery Place," published in *The Horticulturist and Journal of Rural Art and Rural Taste*, Downing described the estate as " ... second ... to no seat in America, for its combination of attractions ... all its varied mysteries of pleasure grounds and lawns, wood and water."[5] In the 1920s and 1930s, Violetta White Delafield created the garden that is still in place today.

Today Montgomery Place is owned by Historic Hudson Valley, a non-profit organization that operates a number of house museums. The property is still a working fruit farm, growing and, in the autumn, selling apples and peaches, as these old estates have done for generations.

Boscobel

Garrison, Putnam County, 1804–8

Boscobel was the dream house of Anglophile States Morris Dyckman (1755–1806), a self-made gentleman and a man of taste in post-Revolutionary America. Despite the aristocratic associations of his surname, Dyckman was the son of a struggling Hudson Valley innkeeper. A Loyalist during the Revolution, he spent eleven years in London in service to the Crown. When amnesty was declared in 1789, he came home to New York, married the young and attractive Elizabeth Corne, and settled on a gentleman's farm in Westchester County. After several disastrous years of illness and financial reversals, Dyckman returned to London in late 1799 to recoup an annuity from the British Army. His claim was successful, and with his new fortune, he was able to build this fashionable house. Before leaving England, he had chosen the name Boscobel, from Boscobel Forest in Shropshire, and shipped a large collection of silver, china, and crystal to New York. No architect has been identified, and it is entirely possible that Dyckman also brought plans for the house back with him.

The Federal style of the south front is derived from several late-eighteenth-century British sources. The wood frame house sits on a high basement of dressed brownstone, like a pedestal, more formal than the fieldstone foundations of many other American country houses. The recessed double loggia under the pediment is Palladian in inspiration,[1] as is the whole composition—a square, freestanding country villa. Although certain elements, including the wooden structure and siding, make it American, in many other ways Boscobel is like an English house. The tripartite windows, known as "Wyatt" windows after the English architect Thomas Wyatt, appear in houses by Robert Adam and other English architects from around 1800. The immense double-hung window sash with large panes recall late-eighteenth-century and Regency houses in England. The extravagant carved-wood swag (or drapery and tassel) on the upper loggia and the swag over the fanlight are closely related to decorative elements in William Pain's architec-

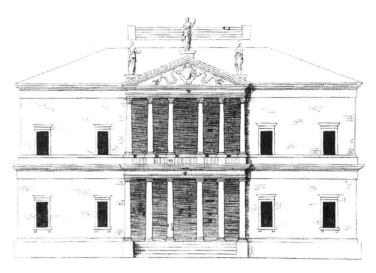

This villa by Andrea Palladio, plate 56 in the second book of the Quattro Libri, *is the distant ancestor of Boscobel's double recessed loggia.*

LEFT: *The staircase and the Palladian window create the architectural climax of the interior of the house.*

tural handbooks of the 1780s and 1790s. Many mantelpiece designs are also from Pain's illustrations.[2]

Late-eighteenth-century English architecture also inspired Charles Bulfinch, but his interpretation was somewhat more conservative than that of the designer of Boscobel. The plan and staircase in Bulfinch's house for Joseph Coolidge Sr. (1791–92) were quite similar to those at Boscobel. Perhaps both Bulfinch and Dyckman had seen the similar (if much grander) staircase by James Wyatt at Heaton Hall in England, a house of 1772.[3]

Boscobel is, however, a unique house, and there are no comparable buildings in the New England or Mid-Atlantic states. In the South, there are several houses with Palladian-inspired double loggias—Jefferson's first design for Monticello (1771–72) and Drayton Hall (1742), outside Charleston, for example. The treatment of the grand staircase at Boscobel, set behind an arcaded screen in a central, square hall, is also very like that of the Chase-Lloyd House (1771–74) in Annapolis.[4]

When he returned from England, Dyckman began plans for the new house, but he died in 1806 and his widow and cousin finished the project on land overlooking Haverstraw Bay in Montrose in 1808. Elizabeth Dyckman furnished the house and

The double parlors exhibit much notable New York Federal furniture.

RIGHT: *The library is the principal and central room of the second floor. It has splendid Hudson River views.*

raised her son, Peter Corne Dyckman, there. After her death, the house passed to Peter and then to his daughter. Subsequent generations and other owners were unable to maintain it, and the house suffered tremendous decline.

In 1955, through the efforts of local preservationists, Boscobel was rescued from demolition, disassembled, and stored for future rebuilding. Many architecturally significant elements—mantelpieces, the great carved swag of the facade, the pediments—which had been removed and sold off, were brought back to prepare for rebuilding on a new site. A gift from Lila Acheson Wallace, cofounder with her husband, DeWitt Wallace, of the Reader's Digest Association, made it possible to acquire a new piece of land in Garrison, about fifteen miles north of the original location, and to resurrect the house.

The reconstructed Boscobel opened in 1961 as a house museum, with rooms filled with eighteenth-century English antiques. To the shock of the curators, a 1806 inventory of the possessions of States Dyckman, discovered in the mid-1970s, revealed that, with the exception of the collection of English china and silver, the original furnishings had all been American. Berry B. Tracy,

then chief curator of the American Wing of the Metropolitan Museum of Art, was retained to determine the appropriate decor and furnishings for the house. His conclusions, now renowned among art and architectural historians, resulted in the de-accessioning of all the English furniture, and the assemblage and installation of the finest collection of New York Federal furniture in existence.[5]

Today, Tracy is recognized as a brilliant curator, but he is also, perhaps more importantly, credited with creating an entirely new idea for house museum exhibitions. Tracy believed that a house museum's interiors should look as they had when the house was new. The workshop of the prominent dealer Israel Sack was engaged exclusively for an entire year to restore and polish the furniture Tracy acquired for Boscobel.[6] The result was immaculate: the veneers and gilding gleamed; there was no fading, no romantic patina. And all the textiles, rugs, and wallpapers were fresh, new reproductions. When the house reopened in 1977, all was as Elizabeth Dyckman would have wanted it to be around 1810. Many visitors thought it seemed too garish, too vibrant, not genteel enough—not enough like a museum full of antique objects. But as an interpretive philosophy, the "Tracy style" has prevailed, and the current curators are striving to maintain it.

The views from the house and garden at Boscobel are among the best on the river. The house faces south from an exceedingly high position. Below is the immense Constitution Marsh. To the west of the marsh, Constitution Island lies in the middle ground, with the Hudson Highlands and West Point beyond. The garden, orchard, lawns, and formal approaches to the house were designed in the late 1950s by Innocenti and Webel of New York. These distinguished grounds, in the mid-twentieth-century estate style, have now become important in American garden history and add greatly to the museum visit.

States Dyckman never saw Boscobel except in his imagination, but it is very much his house. Anglophile and royalist, he was also a product of the new Republican era that permitted such material and aesthetic self-fulfillment.

The main facade in its original Federal guise as conjectured by historian Roger Kennedy. Today the facade is a composite of Federal and Greek Revival elements.

Jacob Rutsen Van Rensselaer House

Claverack, Columbia County, c. 1805

Envision, on the front side of the house, a pair of octagonal drawing rooms of high, airy proportions, positioned side by side, communicating by an elegant double door in the center of the common wall. The Neoclassical mantelpiece in each room faces its counterpart across the axis passing through the double doors. Each facet of each octagon frames a Neoclassical element— an entrance door, an Adamesque mantelpiece, or a window, either exterior or interior or faux and mirrored to reflect the rooms and the view. This pair of rooms seems like a freestanding pavilion, quite French in feeling, and almost completely symmetrical. Behind the octagonal rooms is a center stair hall, flanked by two square rooms, one behind each octagon. Small triangular rooms fill the interstices. The upstairs rooms are aligned with the spaces below, and in the basement, thick stone and brick walls enclose these shapes. The octagons, then, are stacked upon one another, three high.

This is the beautiful and radical arrangement of rooms behind the broad, symmetrical five-bay facade of this house. Outside, the only hints of the delightful surprise to come are the canted corners of the front elevation, which are hardly perceptible at a distance.

The central hall behind the pair of octagonal rooms.

OPPOSITE: *One of the square rooms behind the octagonal rooms, with contemporary floor painting.*

This design, with a conservative facade masking a stylish interior, is eccentric, but there have been other such buildings in New York State. The Hill, built by Henry Walter Livingston, c. 1796–99 and now destroyed, had a similar, but even more recherché, plan, featuring a pair of *oval* drawing rooms. The architectural historian Roger Kennedy believes these two houses, approximately ten miles apart in the center of Columbia County, may have been designed by the French architect Pierre Pharoux.[1] Pharoux is known to have visited Albany and the surrounding countryside in the early 1790s, and he often made schematic plans of houses as thank-you presents for his hosts. Kennedy sur-

mises that such a preliminary design may have been drawn for this house ten years before it was built. About this time, Pharoux did design the LeRay house near Watertown, which also has a pair of octagonal drawing rooms and a plan similar to the Van Rensselaer house. In the mid-1790s, the Livingston family commissioned him to design a whole new town in the French Neoclassical style for a site on the west bank of the Hudson, but it was never built.

Very different from the English-inspired Federal style of New England, the French influence in American Neoclassical architecture in the post-Revolutionary period is a fascinating

*One of the octagonal drawing rooms
is used today as a dining room.*

phenomenon. Through much of the eighteenth century, the Livingstons, the Van Rensselaers, and the other patrician families of New York had used English models, but by the Federal era, many had become Francophiles. French culture was part of the American experience. The language had been taught at Colonial colleges since the mid-eighteenth century, and some Hudson Valley aristocrats had been educated in the French Huguenot school at New Rochelle. From 1790 to 1815, there were many French architects at work in New York, including Joseph-François Mangin, the designer, with John McComb, of New York City Hall, in 1811; and Joseph-Jacques Ramée, who was designing Union College at Schenectady between 1812 and 1815. For some New Yorkers, late-eighteenth-century French Neoclassicism, with its emphasis on abstraction, geometric form, lightness, large windows, and innovative and elegant floor plans, was an antidote to Georgian style, and it was very popular with the Livingstons in particular. Not far from Claverack, several Livingston houses have French associations—not only The Hill, but also Chancellor Robert R. Livingston's Arryl House, formerly adjacent to Clermont, and Montgomery Place.

Originally part of the Van Rensselaer Manor, this part of Columbia County was separated from the feudal jurisdiction of the Manor in 1704 and became Claverack. A 1,000-acre farm was given to Jacob Rutsen Van Rensselaer (1767–1835) in 1803 by his father, Brigadier General Robert Van Rensselaer. The sophisticated, "modern" house Jacob Rutsen built replaced his father's earlier, probably Dutch-style, house on the same site.

Like so many Federal houses, the Van Rensselaer house was altered during the Greek Revival period, probably in the 1840s. The big front porch with its Ionic columns, the transom, sidelights, and architrave of the front door; and the heavy paneled balustrade surmounting the front and sides of the main block of the house are Greek Revival elements, and they change the appearance of the house significantly.

The view from one octagonal room into the other.

OPPOSITE:
The Greek Revival front porch.

PAGES120—121:
The Red Mills of Claverack, on Claverack Creek.

The original block is brick, now painted white over its original yellow. To the rear of this solid, white volume, is a wing added by the Clifford L. Miller family in 1928 in the Colonial Revival style. True to the Colonial Revival, the wing is red brick with white trim, and therefore nicely set off from the earlier Neoclassical house. Miller, who operated a large fruit growing business here, was a leader in the New York State Democratic Party and a Harvard classmate of Franklin Delano Roosevelt. The house has many Roosevelt associations, and the locals still recall FDR speaking from the front porch.

Situated far back from the country highway, the house is surrounded by expansive lawns displaying scores of handsome specimen trees. To the side are nineteenth-century barns, a ten-acre mill pond on Claverack Creek, and an extensive complex of eighteenth- and nineteenth-century mill buildings. These are the "Red Mills" of Claverack, begun in 1767, once a gristmill, where plaster was also made. Although the original house has been altered by its Greek Revival and Colonial Revival "improvements," this entire campus—main house, barns, mill buildings, historic landscape, and mill pond—retains a calm dignity and the serenity it has had now for nearly two centuries.

Cedar Grove:
The Thomas Cole National Historic Site

Catskill, Greene County, 1815

Thomas Cole (1801–1848) is celebrated as the first of the Hudson River School of landscape painters, and an artist who created a new vision for American art. Cedar Grove is a lovely Federal farmhouse, but perhaps its greatest interest lies in its association with Cole from 1836 until his early death in 1848. Unlike Frederic Edwin Church's Olana just across the Hudson, this house was not designed by the painter himself. It is simply where Cole went to live when he married into the resident family, and where he painted, in the house and in two studio buildings across the garden.

Cole's personal story is legendary in the annals of American art. He was the son of English immigrant parents, from Lancashire, who brought their family to the States for a better life around 1818. The Lancashire lad had been an engraver's assistant in Liverpool, and when the family arrived in Philadelphia, he worked again as an engraver. As his parents moved restlessly from Pennsylvania to Ohio to New York, Cole gave art lessons to earn money and learned oil painting around 1820 from an itinerant portraitist. By 1824, already beginning his meteoric rise, Cole was in Philadelphia studying at the Pennsylvania Academy of the Fine Arts, paying close attention to the work of the American landscape painter, Thomas Doughty.

In 1825—a momentous year for Cole—he took up residence in New York City, and for the first time, he went to the Catskill Mountains along the west side of the Hudson to sketch. Cole made his first summer sketching foray up the Hudson as far as the mouth of the Mohawk River; his sketchbook from the trip is his diary, and it includes views in the Catskill Mountains near the village of Catskill, where he was later to live. When the paintings he made from the sketches were exhibited in New York, Cole came immediately to the attention of such established painters as Colonel John Trumbull and Asher B. Durand. These paintings celebrating the wild landscape of New York State, particularly the Catskill Mountains, launched Cole's career and the Hudson River School.

Charles Herbert Moore, Thomas Cole's Cedar Grove, *1868.*

The Thomas Cole National Historic Site

Over the next three summers, Cole traveled up-river from New York City and then back in the fall to exhibit and sell his work to a new generation of American collectors. Cole went to London in 1829, meeting John Constable and J.M.W. Turner and showing his landscapes at the Royal Academy. He traveled to Paris in 1831, where he was disappointed with the old masters in the Louvre, and then to Florence, where he took life drawing classes with the American artist Samuel F.B. Morse and others. By the time he returned to New York in 1832, he was an international artistic celebrity.

By the mid-1830s, Cole was a regular summer visitor to the village of Catskill, where he rented a studio building from the Thomson family, at their farm, Cedar Grove. In 1836, he married Maria Bartow, one of the nieces of the Thomson brothers who had built the graceful yellow farmhouse with a peach-colored front door. The Thomson brothers were both bachelors. One amassed a fortune in South America at the time of the War of 1812, and together they acquired 111 acres along the river and built this house on a hill about a quarter of a mile inland.

In many respects, the high, rectangular, three-bay house is a plain structure, with a conservative plan. Unlike other more stylish New York houses of this period, there are no oval or octagonal rooms, but it does have beautiful triple-hung sash windows extending to the floor in the main rooms and giving onto a piazza that wraps around the south and west elevations and to another porch on the northeast corner. From the piazza there is a splendid view of the Catskills, entirely worthy of Thomas Cole. There is a beauti-

fully designed and constructed open staircase, rising three floors to the attic, in four straight runs, with slender balusters, newels, and handrails crafted from tiger maple. This is the farmhouse of a comfortable upper-middle-class family, not a villa or a family seat.

On the second floor, to the rear of the stair hall is a small north-facing room where Cole painted during the winter, when the studio buildings across the garden were too cold. He is said to have painted his monumental series, *The Course of the Empire*, in this room between 1833 and 1836. About ten years later, the teenaged Frederic Church learned to paint as Cole's student in this room.

Cole and Church went on to have a close and famous friendship. It was Cole the teacher who took Church the student across the river to a high hill with a fine view of the Catskill Mountains. That spot is the place where, in 1870, Church built Olana.

Cole was not a native-born American, and yet he became the most American of painters. His subject matter was sublime nature, and it is not surprising that he was an early environmentalist, deeply suspicious of modern commercial development. Cole's biographer, Ellwood C. Parry III, has written, "His underlying criticism of unbridled belief in material progress and earthly rewards seems unmistakable."[1] Perhaps, as Parry suggests, Cole celebrated the North American landscape as an outsider, and his beautiful paintings were created not only to honor the scenic riches of American nature, but also to warn of the environmental degradation he feared would result from industrial and commercial development in the Hudson River Valley.

Thomas Cole, Mountain Sunrise, Catskill, *1826.*
Courtesy of Berry-Hill Galleries, Inc.

Jasper F. Cropsey, Thomas Cole's Studio, Catskill, New York, *c. 1850.*

Wadsworth Atheneum, Hartford

Eastview

Greenport, Columbia County, c. 1815

This beautiful house was created as a summer place—an American villa, if you will—for a family from the nearby Federal city of Hudson. Although of dazzling design, it was a simple house without many bedrooms, without interior shutters, without many of the accommodations and comforts such a family might have desired in a year-round house. The original owner was Joab Center, about whom little is known. He is reputed to have come from Hartford, Connecticut, to Hudson, where he married a Miss Jenkins. Her family was among the Quaker New Englanders who founded Hudson in 1785 as a new town dedicated to ship-building, whaling, and seafaring. Local legend identifies Center as a retired sea captain. There is no documentation of that livelihood, but he did own a farm in nearby Claverack, where he raised merino sheep. What is obvious, however, is that he must have known and been able to afford a very modish architect for his pleasure pavilion.

Unique in American architecture, this house is famous and loved because of its roofline. Two identical curved, convex, pediments cap identical, two-story, semi-circular porticos on its identical east and west facades. For generations, it has been known locally as the Turtle House because of its shape: a shallow-pitched rectangular roof with full semi-circular ends creates a lozenge-shaped "lid" over the high main block of the house, including the twin bowed pediments.

As surprising as the building appears today, in its original form it was even more dramatic. The original massing of the building is obscured by alterations to the two low, lateral wings that flank the "turtle" block. The wings were once a single story, but their roofs were raised in the Greek Revival period to create second-story bedrooms. As a result, some of the volumetric drama of the juxtaposition of the tall central block with the lower wings was lost. At the same time, the two odd semi-circular wooden projections on the lateral sides of the main block were greatly diminished.

The plan of the house is elegant and simple, and it demonstrates the tremendous freedom that could be achieved in American Federal houses. On the main floor, the primary and central block accommodates a pair of adjoining drawing rooms, identical in plan, rectangular, but with semi-circular ends. These rooms, together 40 feet in length, and with 12-foot ceilings, are linked by a generous opening that was originally fitted with a pair of eight-panel, hinged doors. Each room has three floor-length windows in the curved end wall and a Greek Revival mantelpiece of veined gray marble. Stacked above, on the second floor, is a pair of bedrooms of the same size and shape, each also with three windows in its curved end.

In each of the rectangular flanking wings, originally, there was an additional, squarish room, and a small stairhall. The wings had two exterior doors, one on the east, one on the west, giving out to the semi-circular porticos. In this plan, therefore, there were four entrances, all equal in importance; there was no central hall and no important staircase to the upper floor—the layout was as innovative and revolutionary as the massing of the building itself.

The originality of the design has made it seem *sui generis* to many observers, but there was an interesting precedent in the work of Charles Bulfinch. His house for James Swan in Dorchester, Massachusetts, about 1796, had a similar plan with a semi-circular projection in its center block, surrounded by a curved piazza, and a pair of low flanking wings.[1]

Joab Center owned four lots here for a total of forty acres. Forty acres did not make much of a farm, but it did create a nice country estate. The house was sited on a flat place above a steep slope, with a view to the east toward the farmland of central Columbia County and then to the Berkshire Hills beyond.

James Vanderpoel House

Kinderhook, Columbia County, c. 1819

The James Vanderpoel house sits on Broad Street, just off to the side of the village green in Kinderhook. The house faces southeast and is about 120 feet back from the street. Kinderhook is one of America's most significant and charming old towns because so much of the historic fabric is intact, and there has been very little inappropriate development. The Vanderpoel house is a vernacular example of American Federal domestic architecture, with several sophisticated elements.

The town is located on Kinderhook Creek, a wide Hudson River tributary, and, according to some historians, it owes its name to Henry Hudson. In the autumn of 1609, on his voyage from New York harbor to just south of the future site of Albany, Hudson reportedly saw Indian children playing at the mouth of the creek, and he called the creek and the place Kinderhook, or "children's corner." Whether or not this is true, just a few years later, in a famous map dated 1614–16, Adrian Block labeled the creek "Kinderhook." This is one of the first places named in New York history.[1]

Close to the river, on a navigable stream, and surrounded by fertile river-valley lands, Kinderhook has long been an affluent and prominent place. The first land purchased from the Indians was bought about 1650 by the Patroon Kiliaen Van Rensselaer. In 1689, thirty-one "proprietors" received a township charter, and Kinderhook was separated from the great feudal patroonship of the Van Rensselaers.

James Vanderpoel (1787–1843) was a prosperous, young, obviously modern-thinking lawyer, who with his wife, Anna Doll Vanderpoel, lived in Kinderhook and later in Albany. When the house was built, the Vanderpoels were in their late thirties, and they were part of the old Dutch world. James Vanderpoel was also a public servant, and a member of the Albany political circle of Martin Van Buren, a fellow resident of Kinderhook. Shortly after their house was built, their portraits were painted by the now-famous itinerant artist Ammi Phillips. The paintings are now in the collection of the Albany Institute of History and Art.

Kinderhook is only eighteen miles southeast of Albany, and about the same distance from Hudson. Both cities influenced the Vanderpoel story. The city of Hudson was founded in 1785 by New England and Nantucket fishermen and shipbuilders as a "safe haven" waterfront and shipbuilding town, on the Atlantic in a sense, because of easy sailing down the river to New York harbor. Hudson became very rich in the early nineteenth century, as many whaling ships set sail from this port, even as far as to the Antarctic and the Bering Sea.[2]

By the time the Vanderpoel house was built, there were important Federal houses in Albany, and good examples in Hudson. These houses, breaking with the heavier Georgian style, were a new American development. They were directly related to the houses of Bulfinch and McIntire, and derived many design elements from English buildings of Robert Adam. For a conservative, country town like Kinderhook, still depending on an agricultural economic base, the Vanderpoel house must have been a dazzling modern addition.

The building is a simple rectangle measuring 53 feet across the front and 40 feet deep, with a five-bay symmetrical design on the east front, and a nearly identical rear facade. The two-story building with pedimented gable ends is set on a high fieldstone foundation. The brick on the east and north sides is laid in Flemish bond, while the pattern on the back and south sides is common bond. There is evidence that the brick was originally stained dark red with a white line painted on the mortar. The windows are double hung with six-over-six sash. At the center of the second floor is a three-part, vernacular Venetian window with a leaded fanlight similar to that over the main door. Originally a wooden roof balustrade crossed the house horizontally, and then climbed the gable ends to completely surround the roof.

The most notable feature of the interior is the exceptionally beautiful hallway, with its elegant cantilevered and curving stair. The light is dramatic in this room, falling in from the leaded sidelights of the street and garden doors, and down the stairs from the triple windows at both ends of the upstairs hall. A large, nearly elliptical opening above the stair creates a two-story space. The staircase is reminiscent of several in Bulfinch houses, but in Kinderhook, the carpenter may have followed the drawings and geometrical formulas in the architectural handbooks of Asher Benjamin. The house also has beautifully designed and carved wooden architraves around and over important interior doorways. These are Adamesque in spirit with unusual details including applied decorations made of lead.

The house was purchased in 1925 by the Columbia County Historical Society for their headquarters and for restoration as a house museum. The restoration and furnishing were carried out in the late 1920s, a period of fervent interest in Colonial Revival architecture and decoration. Today most of the 1920s work has been remedied or swept away, and in response to a new and exceptionally thorough furnishings plan by the preservation architects Mesick-Cohen-Waite of Albany, a new era is beginning. The Historical Society intends to restore the house to the period of

Ammi Phillips, James Vanderpoel *and*
Anna Doll Vanderpoel, *c. 1822. The*
portraits originally hung in the house.
Albany Institute of History & Art

OPPOSITE: *This parlor set up as a dining room*
is currently being redecorated, and the English
overmantel will be replaced soon with an
American object.

Vanderpoel occupancy. The hallway, now richly painted and wall-papered, with its beautifully designed floor-cloth, represents the style that the architects and curators believe reflects more closely the way the Vanderpoels lived.

The period landscape and garden setting of this house has disappeared. Old photographs show a fine wooden fence on the street side of the property, an informal allée of sugar maples flanking the central walk, a picturesque grove of American elms at the north end of the house, and wooden board-and-batten Gothic revival outbuildings placed symmetrically to the sides and rear of the house. An historic landscape report from the office of R.M. Toole of Saratoga Springs recommends the replanting of the kitchen garden and orchard. Since the original garden scheme has now been lost, it will be wonderful some day for visitors to return to the Vanderpoels' charming village house, when the garden and landscape have been restored.

Edgewater

Barrytown, Dutchess County, c. 1825

Probably built in 1825, rather late in the Federal period, and just at a moment when Greek Revival temple fronts were beginning to be seen on important houses, Edgewater has a major temple front, but it is not Greek Revival. It is thoroughly Federal. This monumental porch derives not from ancient Greek models, but from the Roman temples of antiquity. It owes the style of its great Roman Revival portico to the passions of Thomas Jefferson. Jefferson had succeeded Benjamin Franklin as ambassador to France in the 1780s. He had fallen under the spell of the ancient Roman architecture in the south of France, especially the famous Maison Carée at Nîmes, a building of the first century A.D. To his friend the Comtesse de Tessé, Jefferson wrote in 1784, "Here I am … gazing whole hours at the Maison Carée, like a lover at his mistress."[1] By 1785, Jefferson was already designing his first monumental Roman Revival temple front—the Virginia State Capitol. Over the next twenty years, Jefferson designed Roman-inspired porticos for buildings such as Monticello and the University of Virginia, and recommended them to friends, including James Madison, who added a monumental portico to his Virginia house, Montpelier, in 1793.

Understanding Edgewater as a Federal-period house with its major design element of Roman, French, and Jeffersonian inspiration places it among the group of Livingston and Van Rensselaer houses of the early nineteenth century with French architectural connections. Edgewater was built, close to the river, only a few feet above water level, for Margaret Livingston Brown, the granddaughter of Margaret Beekman Livingston, mistress of Clermont. She was the wife of Captain Loundes Brown of Charleston, South Carolina. The land associated with the house was deeded to Margaret Brown in late 1824, by her father, and the date of the house is believed to be 1825.

The original floor plan has much in common with Montgomery Place. The main entrance has always been on the east rather than the riverfront. The original house is a large

The entrance or east front (ABOVE) and the great Roman Revival portico overlooking the river (OPPOSITE).

OPPOSITE, BELOW: *A nineteenth-century view of the house and its riverside setting.*

rectangle, situated on a north-south axis, and as at Montgomery Place, there is a pair of principal rooms adjoining and occupying the entire western facade. Here at Edgewater the room used as a living room today is on the north end of this main block and has three bays; the room to the south is the dining room, and it has two bays. The Federal details in these rooms are typical of the 1820s, and many are similar to those at the Hart-Cluett house in Troy of just two years later.

What is unique among Hudson River houses of this period is the Roman Doric, hexastyle, two-story portico on the riverfront. This temple front originally stood on a high Roman-style base or "podium." Totally unlike a Roman temple, however, the portico is applied to the long side of the building. It is tempting to think that

The Federal staircase amidst Federal furnishings of great quality. Many Livingston and Donaldson paintings and objects have been reassembled here.

the Browns may have built a plainer Federal house facing the river and later changed the roofline and added the portico. Supporting the idea that such changes may have been made, the current owner of the house believes that the elegant curving and cantilevered staircase, a throw-back to Bulfinch's Boston staircases of this design, c. 1800, is the second Federal stair in roughly the same location.[2]

The high podium on which the portico stood was buried under two levels of grass terrace in the 1850s by the architect Alexander Jackson Davis. This major design change brings the lawn up much closer to the level of the portico floor, and to some extent "de-Romanizes" the house. By this date, the house was owned by Robert Donaldson, a native of North Carolina and a well-known aesthete and sponsor of the then-new Picturesque Revival styles such as the Gothic and the Italianate. Donaldson brought in his friend Davis, and they added "new" Italianate elements seen in the house today. In 1854, Davis created a new north-south axis through the old Federal house, on the river side. He did not alter the Federal rooms, but he added a wing for an octagonal library with a skylight and bay windows on the north,

The drawing and dining rooms are the principal spaces of the original house. They contain a collection of New York furniture of the early 1800s, much of it by Duncan Phyfe.

and a large walk-in bay window on the south. By aligning the entrances to these one-story additions with the original large opening between the two main rooms of the Federal house, Davis created a grand enfilade parallel to the river. Davis also stuccoed the old brick house, scored the stucco to resemble cut stone, and had it marbleized. These details and additions, like the grass terraces Davis used to disguise the podium, also de-emphasize the Roman-ness of the house, making it more like the Italianate villa Donaldson was probably hoping to achieve.[3] The monumental temple front, with its simplified entablature, reflecting light from the great tidal river, was not to be turned into a "picturesque" style, however. Its classicism is too strong, and Davis's work seems entirely subsidiary to the strength of the original architecture.

Edgewater has always been a private house. At one point in the mid-twentieth century, it was lived in by the writer Gore Vidal, who conducted a bohemian social life in this elegant setting. The current owner is a distinguished financier who has assembled a significant collection of Duncan Phyfe furniture and other decorative arts of the periods of Margaret Livingston Brown and the Donaldsons. There are many Livingston and Donaldson family objects and paintings back in the house today.

No other Hudson River house relates to the water quite as this one does. The property is a series of peninsulas extending about two hundred feet into the river. The house sits on the largest of these projections of land, and the river surrounds the house on three sides. There is a strong stone sea wall protecting the perimeter of the site, and ancient basswood, willow, and black locust trees follow the shoreline and enhance the lawns. The house and this combination of topographical elements are so glorious that the spectacular view across the river to the Catskills is almost irrelevant.

Hart-Cluett Mansion

Troy, Rensselaer County, 1827

lbany is an old place of habitation, dating back to the earliest European settlement of the Hudson River Valley, but Troy, just seven miles upriver and across, on the east bank, is a post-Revolutionary town. First called Vanderheyden, the early village had its rectangular street grid laid out in 1781, and the city of Troy was established in 1789.

At this place on the Hudson, three powerful streams from the east tumble into the river, falling downhill some two hundred feet. These tributaries provided the waterpower early on to run major grist and lumber mills, and their products were easily shipped down the Hudson from Troy's warehouses and docks. Textiles also became a major industry, linen collars followed, then shirts. Iron works were plentiful, and important early American industrial companies, such as the shirt manufacturer Cluett, Peabody & Co. and the Burden Iron Works, made Troy a rich industrial city.

The fine white Westchester marble house at 59 Second Street was built in 1827 for one great Trojan business family, and subsequently lived in by another. It has been operated as a museum by the Rensselaer County Historical Society since the 1950s. Thanks to a strong local community of architectural historians, this distinguished town house is one of New York's most studied, most documented domestic buildings. The buildings most closely related to this sophisticated house are the Federal and Greek Revival houses of Manhattan from the late 1820s and 1830s. In *The Marble House on Second Street: Biography of a Town House and Its Occupants, 1825–2000*, architectural historians Douglas Bucher and Walter Richard Wheeler make a persuasive case for attributing the design of the Hart-Cluett house to Martin E. Thompson, who was working in New York City and Troy in this period. Today, Thompson is best known as the designer of the Second Branch Bank of the United States, 1822–26, also of white Westchester marble, and now the principal architectural wonder of the American Wing of the Metropolitan Museum of Art.

TOP: *An elaborate town house doorway, from Minard Lafever,* The Young Builder's General Instructor, *1829.*

RIGHT: *The Second Street facade is faced with Westchester marble. The fine ironwork was characteristic of the best Albany and Troy buildings in this period.*

The Federal interiors are notable for their carvings and the cantilevered staircase.

The house may have been commissioned by the New York businessman William Howard, who gave it to his daughter, Betsey Howard Hart (1798–1886), and her husband, the local Trojan entrepreneur and business leader Richard P. Hart (1780–1843). This family lived very luxuriously in the house—at first with their 14 children—until Mrs. Hart's death. They furnished the house with New York City classical furnishings, some attributed to Duncan Phyfe, but later, after considerable mid-century redecoration, with high style Rococo Revival furnishings. Mrs. Hart was a gifted businesswoman herself. Running the family investments for four decades after her husband's death, she kept detailed records of her trips to New York City, and her purchases of all kinds, including furnishings and decorations. Her papers are in the care of The

Rensselaer County Historical Society, and because of them a great deal is known about the way people have lived in this house.

The George Cluett family, of the local collar and shirt-making business, bought the house in 1893; they were succeeded by his nephew, Albert Cluett, and his family in 1910. The Harts and Cluetts were always among the "first families" of Troy, and the list of their civic involvements, charities, churches, schools, and institution-building activities demonstrates that they were generous and altruistic.

The house is four bays wide, three stories tall, sitting on a high basement. The proportions are very large, the main rooms being over 13 feet high and the windows with double-hung sash being nearly nine feet tall. According to contemporary documents, the

The central hallway looking from the front door into the house.

white marble came up the Hudson in April 1826, as soon as the ice had broken up and the river was open for the season. The house would have taken probably a year to build and might have been ready for the family to occupy in 1827 by May 1, "the traditional moving day"[1]

The elaborate main doorway, the rusticated blocks around the doorway and the basement windows, the heavy keystones over the basement windows, the classical moldings of the window architraves, the beautifully designed and crafted iron work—these are the refinements of design and construction that set this house apart from others upstate and make it comparable to fine New York City houses of the same era, and even London town houses of a few years earlier. The architect, presumably Martin Thompson, drew upon eighteenth-century English architectural books for inspiration, including Abraham Swan's 1757 *A Collection of Designs in Architecture*. The four-bay floor plan is similar to Swan floorplans, and details such as the rosette design for the prominent carved corner blocks used in door and window architraves throughout the interior may have been derived from illustrations in Swan's *The British Architect*, published in Philadelphia in 1775.[2]

The interiors of the house are currently being refurbished to the period of the mid-nineteenth century. The rooms retain their original marble mantelpieces, original decorative plaster work of great detail and quality, and fine carved woodwork thought to be by the well-known Albany and New York City woodworker Henry Farnham. Farnham is celebrated for his beautiful work with Albany architect Philip Hooker on the still-extant Albany Academy, 1815–17.

Originally, the house was freestanding with a deep garden next door, to the south, extending from the street to the alley way behind. The side, or south, facade of the house was, therefore, a garden front, with an important side entrance. When the Cluett family bought the house, they sold the garden. The house was built on this site does not abut the white marble house, but it blocks the side entrance, and the light and air from the south.

This old section of downtown Troy, just adjacent to the historic campus of Russell Sage College, is as quiet and purely residential as it always has been. Walking these narrow streets, block after block of brick house fronts not much changed for 175 years, it is a delight to come upon the sparkling white marble house at 59 Second Street.

CHAPTER 5

THE GREEK REVIVAL WAVE

In the 1820s and 1830s, the influence of ancient Greece eclipsed that of Rome in American architecture. Greek archeology had first excited interest in the late eighteenth century and, in Europe at least, even threatened the primary position long held by Roman precedents. The tide began to turn with the 1787 publication of *The Antiquities of Athens* by James Stuart and Nicholas Revett, which included a reconstruction of the Parthenon and measured drawings of Greek columns, capitals, and entablatures. The Greek Revival style was first articulated in America in a powerful way in 1818, when the architect William Strickland built his second Bank of the United States in Philadelphia.

When the populist Andrew Jackson was elected President in 1828, the American middle class was eager for new ideas that would separate its thinking from that of the patrician circles that had dominated the country in the post-Revolutionary period. Americans were captivated by the contemporary Greek war of independence and the connection between American democracy and that of ancient Greece. Industrialization was bringing prosperity, which, combined with a romantic quest for individualism, created a market for the new style, a Neoclassicism without aristocratic associations.

The Greek Revival became enormously popular, its spread made possible by inexpensive carpenters and builders handbooks. By 1827, Asher Benjamin's *The American Builder's Companion* had delineated the classical orders for carpenters to copy. Minard Lafever's *Modern Builder's Guide*, published in 1833, gave designs for entablatures, pilasters, architraves, doors, and windows—some details deriving directly from Greek sources, some from the work of high-style architects like Ithiel Town, and some invented. All could be constructed by local carpenters.

Greek Revival architecture, in all of its monumentality, lent itself very naturally to masonry public buildings, courthouses, banks, and churches, but when rendered in wood, the style became ubiquitous in house design in the eastern United States. The familiar elements are temple fronts in Doric or Ionic orders; monumental pilasters at the corners of the main block; wide Doric entablatures running across the long elevations; large double- or triple-hung windows; "eye-brow" windows on second or third stories, often placed within the frieze element of the entablature; pilasters and heavy lintels as door surrounds and mantelpieces. A Greek Revival house could be masonry, but wood-frame construction was more typical. It was at the level of the farmhouse, as well as the country church and courthouse, that the style became a national movement, and the Greek Revival style that is loved and revered today for its American-ness, is not that of monumental public buildings, but the white clapboard of thousands of humble farmhouses and simple churches.

The Greek Revival took hold in the urban town houses of New York City, too, but more vigorously in the middle-sized buildings in the newer towns and settlements springing up in central and western New York State. By contrast, the Hudson River Valley had become by this time an established center of culture and architectural tradition. In this setting, the Greek Revival blended in with earlier styles and was also counter-balanced by the Picturesque Revival styles that were emerging in the 1840s. Here the force of the Greek Wave was somewhat diminshed by newer and older cultural forces.

Oakcliff

Crescent, Saratoga County, c. 1840

Facing south from the bluffs of the Mohawk River, Oakcliff has a panoramic view of the juncture of the Mohawk, the Hudson, and the Erie Canal. The Canal opened this part of the upper Hudson River Valley to rapid settlement and development, and the Greek Revival spread westward like wildfire from just this point and this date. Built for Judge Duncan McMartin, this archetypal temple-front house has monumental, two-story Doric porticos on both ends of the main 1840s section. The wing on the right was expanded and altered in the 1860s and again in the 1890s.

A plate from Modern Builder's Guide *by Minard Lafever. Designs such as this were primitively rendered by local carpenters such as those who created the west front of the Silvernail Homestead about 1840.*

Silvernail Homestead

Ancram, Columbia County, c. 1795–1840

Standing close to a country road, by a tiny stream, the Silvernail Homestead was built in a hollow for good access to water and shelter from the wind. Today on the flanks of the surrounding hills, there is verdant farmland; on the summits there is woodland and forest where generations ago farmers stopped plowing because such hills are hard on horses and men; in the dales there are streams and swamps. The hills are glacial till, full of gravel and iron ore. The swamps are luxuriant, with willow and alder and abundant wildlife. This is the typical landscape of central and southern Columbia County, little changed from the days of Livingston Manor.

The hamlet of Ancram, two miles to the north of this farm, had been a strong Livingston center for generations, the site of a powerful mill on the river called the Roeliff Janssen Kill, and also near rich iron ore deposits. The great Livingston houses are on and near the Hudson, but here, twenty miles inland, the mill workers and the farmers were mostly poor. Probably because their houses were not well constructed, few of them remain.

The house from the south showing the kitchen wing, which may be older than the main front.

The Silvernails (the name was originally "Silbernagel") were a German refugee family from the Palatinate, a province of Bavaria, in the Rhineland. The founder of the American branch, Adam Silbernagel, had come to America around 1720 in the German Palatine immigration that had begun in 1710 under British sponsorship. Victims of religious persecution, and fleeing from the armies of Louis XIV, the Palatines had ended up in London, unwanted. The British government's intention was to banish them to New York and to put them to work manufacturing pitch tar and other ship stores. The first 2,500 Palatines were settled in Columbia County in a kind of refugee camp known as Germantown, a 6,000 acre plot bought by Queen Anne of England from Robert Livingston in 1710.[1] The scheme did not work. The Palatines were farmers who hated their pitch task, and they ran away from the colony. Some established the town of Herkimer on the Mohawk River, and others, including the Silbernagels, stayed in this part of the Hudson to farm as tenants for the Livingstons.

By 1795, the Silbernagels had Anglicized their name, and John Silvernail (1742–1811) owned what old maps identify as a 224-acre farm, so it seems he had established a freehold.[2] The family must have been quite prosperous by the 1840s, when their old house was expanded and a complete set of Greek Revival elements was applied to the interior and exterior. Since then, this has been a large, L-shaped clapboard house. The plan is very simple: two large square rooms, each twenty feet by twenty feet, flank central halls downstairs and up. A kitchen wing extends to the rear; lean-tos line the rear side of the house, testifying to use by large families.

The whole front section may have been built in the 1840s since the Greek detailing "fits" very well on these elevations, but

BELOW: *The south parlor with Egyptian Revival details.*

RIGHT: *The hallway and the north parlor. The floor-to-ceiling height here is only 7 feet 1 inch.*

there is also reason to believe that this block was a Federal house onto which the Greek Revival layer was applied. As is the case in many wood vernacular houses, so much reworking took place in the nineteenth century that it is difficult, if not impossible, to reconstruct the history.

Everything about this house is idiosyncratic. All of the interior woodwork shows the hand of the maker, perhaps too clearly. Every room has a different design in the door and window trim, and many measurements are off from one side of a door to the other. In low-ceilinged rooms, which seem to antedate the 1840s work, there are the heaviest imaginable architraves framing doors and windows, and the juxtaposition of the low spaces and the heavy architecture makes the carpentry feel like folk art. There are even elements of the Egyptian Revival style, a variation on Greek Revival, with some architraves battered outward as they descend to the floor.

The country carpenters who "made" the 1840s house were profoundly influenced by Lafever's *Modern Builder's Guide*, copying and adapting Greek ideas. Many design elements typical of Greek Revival style farmhouses are present: eyebrow windows incorporated into wide entablatures on the exterior; monumental pilasters at the corners, "supporting" the entablatures, just as stone elements are related to one other in ancient Greek buildings; gable-

end pediments paneled with flush boards and deeply beveled moldings; recessed and paneled aprons under the windows of the first floor, both outside and in; and a plethora of double-hung windows.

The most striking Greek Revival element is the over-scaled entablature above the long front porch on the west front. This heavy Doric feature is supported by six square pillars, which are asymmetrically spaced to correspond with the asymmetry in the windows of the facade. The not-quite centrally positioned main doorway has a door of two "leaves," and sidelights but no transom because of the low ceiling heights inside. The whole entry ensemble is recessed behind the front plane of the house and framed by a wide, "shouldered" architrave.

It seems that there were no fireplaces here in the 1840s, although there is evidence that there had been in the earlier house, and two have been added back in modern times. By 1840, cast-iron stoves and even convection-air furnaces heated houses more efficiently than traditional fireplaces. Folk art it may have been, but this was also a "modern" house when it was built.

The Silvernail family spread all around this section of the county, and various roads and hamlets are named for them. This farm descended from the Silvernails to the Strever Poole family through the female Silvernail line after almost 125 years. The Pooles kept much of the original farm intact and in the family until 1964.

Among all writers on American architecture, William H. Pierson Jr. provides the most insightful framework for understanding buildings like this: "The Greek Revival was irrational and sentimental, and flourished at every level of American society. . . . Indeed, in the hands of the local carpenters it permeated every corner of the land to blossom into one of the most remarkable flowerings of folk art in Western history."[3]

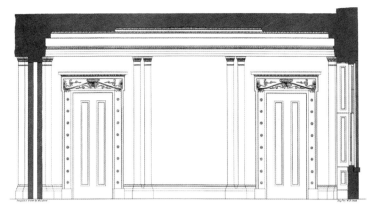

Minard Lafever's design sourcebooks recommended elaborate Greek Revival interior door surrounds. Vernacular versions are found in the Huntting House.

LEFT: *The Greek Revival main house was added onto the "wing" at the right.*

Samuel Huntting House

Stanford, Dutchess County, c. 1840

The Bird House

Stanford, Dutchess County, c. 1839

D istributed among several rural townships, in a loose cluster in central Dutchess County, are at least ten Greek Revival houses and one church attributed by local architects and historians to a prolific master carpenter/designer, Nathaniel Lockwood Jr. (1796–1843). Originally part of the "Great Nine Partners Patent" of 1697 and the "Little Nine Partners Patent" of 1706, this section of Dutchess County was home to a large Quaker community in the years after the Revolutionary War, although the Hunttings, who arrived in 1783 from East Hampton, Long Island, seem to have been Presbyterian.

The large yellow farmhouse known as the Huntting House is one of the least altered of the Lockwood houses. Its form—a three-bay, two-and-a-half-story rectangle, with a pedimented gable end facing the road—appears throughout New York and New England, but this particular example is larger and grander than most. It is sheathed in clapboard with monumental pilasters at all four corners. In this case, the classical entablature that surrounds the house is not as bold or as developed as it can be, but the

The door architraves and ceiling cornices here are much more elaborate than those in most 1840s farmhouses.

triangular pediment is highly detailed with muscular moldings and a large triangular attic window with diamond-shaped panes. This type of triangular window is also seen in other houses attributed to Lockwood.

The main block of the Huntting house has the shape, massing, and roof-pitch of a Greek temple, but as in most farmhouses of this period, there is no columned portico. This is a temple for the common man. The low wing to the right is the older, original house, probably from the late eighteenth century, onto which the Greek Revival block was added. The Greek section has very large six-over-six sash windows, a massive front porch with square pillars, instead of round columns, and a heavy entablature. A porch with similar elements was added to the front of the older wing, presumably at the time of the 1840s building project.

The hand of designer/builder Lockwood is particularly to be seen in the heavy pediments, the "paneled" pilasters, and the distinctive design of the main entrance sidelights and square transom. In addition, the "gathered-lances" porch railing design is seen on several of his houses, as well. His interior elements include a recognizable turned newel post of mahogany, Lafever-style door and window architraves, and a handsomely detailed cornice in all of the main first floor rooms. This house had a personal association for Lockwood, who is said to have built it as a wedding present for his daughter Anna at the time of her marriage to Samuel Huntting's son, Lewis Dibble Huntting.

The plan is of the "side hall" variety, with two large square rooms to the left of the stair hall on each floor. The generous proportions, high ceilings, and fine quality of the design and craftsmanship set this house apart from most New York farmhouses of this type.

Lockwood's most famous building is the beautiful Presbyterian church at Smithfield, with a temple front in the Ionic order. His temple-front houses are unusual for their scale. They

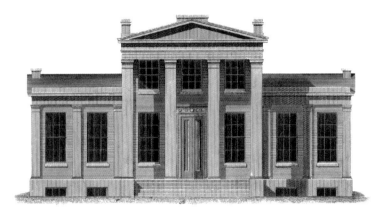

Minard Lafever promoted the temple front flanked by low wings as a stylish house elevation. The Bird House (OPPOSITE) is a local version of this design.

are very heavy and massive in design, but they are not very large, demonstrating the versatility of the Greek Revival format.[1]

Lockwood's houses with temple fronts reveal that this form did not lend itself easily to house expansion. In these houses, the columned porticos and two Greek Revival rooms were grafted onto the fronts of older houses without altering the vernacular floor plan. These are hybrid houses that may reflect the thrifty nature of the Quaker farmers for whom they were built.

The Bird House, only a few miles over the hills from the Huntting House, is one of these hybrid houses. With its weighty Doric, pedimented portico and a pair of one-story wings, it is a good example of Lockwood's temple-front houses and the popular Greek Revival type of a central, two-story temple flanked by low wings.

Nathaniel Lockwood Jr. is unknown outside these towns in rural Dutchess County, and the story of his work remains to be documented. As Talbot Hamlin, the great American scholar of the Greek Revival, has written, "this architecture was necessarily various, changing from region to region . . . as the local culture directed. Thus its roots thrust deeply into local history, and the research which shall make clear its true growth and accomplishment must be local research."[2]

CHAPTER 6

PICTURESQUE REVIVAL STYLES NATIVE TO THE HUDSON

New York architectural taste in the three decades before the Civil War was profoundly influenced, perhaps even dictated, by three men: the novelist Washington Irving, the architectural writer Andrew Jackson Downing, and the architect Alexander Jackson Davis.

Irving was the pioneer: his house, Sunnyside, was underway by 1835. Irving had been to visit Sir Walter Scott in his Tudor Revival house in Scotland, and he brought back home to New York an element of British taste, even as he was also designing the architectural pendant to the Dutch colonial themes of his fiction. At nearly the same moment, Andrew Jackson Downing was importing British ideas in his published work. Downing wrote four books between 1841 and 1850, all concerned with landscape design and the design of American country houses, and the Hudson Valley was his laboratory. Downing was a follower of the slightly earlier English writer on the same set of subjects, J.C. Loudon, also an insistent exponent of the Picturesque in architecture. Downing hated the Greek Revival and "those architects who give us copies of the temple of Theseus, with its high, severe, colonnades, for dwelling."[1]

Downing was a close friend of, and kindred spirit to, Alexander Jackson Davis. Davis could design in any style. His Greek Revival works are visionary masterpieces (for example, the United States Custom House, 1833, now Federal Hall Memorial, in Manhattan), but most of all he loved the Gothic Revival. By the 1850s, Gothic style had been joined by the Italianate, another new idea from Europe, and Downing and Davis promoted that development as well.

The Hudson River houses in this chapter are all related to the three men who shaped the Picturesque Revival movement—Irving designed one, Davis designed two, and Downing's published works created the context for all of them.

It is significant that three of these houses—Sunnyside, Lyndhurst, and Nuits—were built close to one another and within an easy commute of New York City. Irving was a celebrity by the time he built Sunnyside, and although he hated the coming of the railroad up the east bank of the river, it was his lifeline to New York City and his friends there, and to Europe. For the owners of Lyndhurst and Nuits, New York City was home, and these houses were weekend and summer retreats. By the 1850s, the easy transportation in this part of the Hudson Valley made Westchester County fashionable and even suburban. A new era was at hand.

Henry Delamater House
Rhinebeck, Dutchess County, 1844

Designed by Alexander Jackson Davis, this "cottage villa" in the Gothic Revival style, also referred to as "Hudson River Bracketed," is a wonderful example of the Gothic cottage rendered in wood. This kind of house was heavily promoted by Andrew Jackson Downing in his architectural handbooks and widely built throughout New York State and the Northeast. The board-and-batten siding, fanciful verge-boards, pointed arches, bay windows, and decorative verandas, all combine to create a storybook house, which sits on a main street in the village of Rhinebeck.

Sunnyside

Tarrytown, Westchester County, 1835–47

Washington Irving (1783–1859) bought a diminutive house on this riverfront site in 1835, as a retreat from his life as an international celebrity. Expanding and transforming it, Irving was his own architect, helped by a friend and neighbor, the landscape painter and builder George Harvey, who had already created a picturesque cottage for himself nearby. Irving wanted a house that felt antique, where he would be ensconced in a style reminiscent of the old Dutch scenes of his fiction, but he also wanted to incorporate elements of Abbotsford, the Gothic and Tudor Revival country house of Sir Walter Scott in southern Scotland.

He achieved it all. By 1836, his cottage in the Dutch Colonial, Tudor, and Gothic Revival styles was completed—and it was considered trendsetting, even by the professional designers Alexander Jackson Davis and Andrew Jackson Downing. Surveying its elements, the stepped gables are characteristic of both Dutch and Gothic Revival, while the chimneystacks and the casement windows are Tudor Revival. In 1847, with the addition of a Spanish tower, Hispano-Moresque Revival style became part of the mix. Since then, all of these antiquarian and pictorial elements have been blended into the fabric of a wisteria-covered cottage nestled into a cozy spot on the river that may easily be confused with Irving's fictional Sleepy Hollow.

Washington Irving's small study.

OPPOSITE: *The narrow central hall seen from the front door.*

By the mid 1830s, the picturesque styles of the Romantic Revival movement—antithetical in almost all respects to the increasingly pervasive Greek Revival—were beginning to capture the imagination of the Hudson River Valley. J.C. Loudon's extensive treatise on Romantic style, *Encyclopedia of Cottage, Farm, and Villa Architecture,* had appeared in 1833, and the Italian villa style, already established in England, was attracting American designers. In 1838, Alexander Jackson Davis published *Rural Residences,* often seen as the beginning of American picturesque architecture. Davis had asked Irving to write the preface, but he never produced the piece. Still, the episode underscores the influence of Irving's aesthetic.

Irving and his house do appear in Downing's *Treatise on the Practice of Landscape Gardening and Rural Architecture,* 1841, which describes Sunnyside as "almost the beau ideal of a cottage ornée." Downing notes approvingly that the cottage is "quaint," is decorated with "ancient and venerable ornaments," and is surrounded by "foot-paths ingeniously contrived, so as sometimes to afford secluded walks, and at others to allow fine vistas of the broad expanse of river scenery."[1]

Born in New York City, Washington Irving was educated as a lawyer, traveled extensively abroad, and worked for the United States government in diplomatic posts in London and Madrid. He made his reputation as a uniquely American literary genius by mining New York Colonial history as the source of his fiction. Irving celebrated early American character and scenery, especially that of his home territory, the Hudson River Valley and the Catskill Mountains. He had a wide acquaintance in literary and artistic circles, including the painter Thomas Cole, with whom he shared a love of the Valley's wild scenery and unspoiled nature. Since the two were early practitioners of the new romanticism, it seems somehow emblematic that Irving completed his house and Cole moved to Catskill in the same year, 1836.

Somewhat older than his soul mates, Davis, Downing, and Cole, Irving may be seen as a transitional figure and an early

PAGES 180–81: *The south front reveals the eclecticism of the house with its Dutch stepped gables and the Moresque tower on the right.*

thinker about American Romanticism. Long before he and Cole were exploring Hudson River scenery and introducing Romantic aesthetics to America, Irving had tasted Hudson River life on a visit to the Livingstons in August 1812. While there, he dined with Janet Montgomery at Montgomery Place and with Chancellor Livingston at Clermont. Perhaps it was on this visit, too, that he first conceived the Catskill Mountain tale "Rip Van Winkle," published in 1819 in *The Sketch Book of Geoffrey Crayon, Gent.* It is tempting to think that the idea for Rip might have come to Irving as he discussed New York State history with the Chancellor.[2]

Sunnyside is such a celebrated place and house museum that it is surprising to discover what a tiny cottage it is. A lifelong bachelor, Irving lived here with several members of his family, but before the Spanish tower was built (with more bedrooms), the house had only four rooms downstairs and six tiny bedrooms, under the eaves, upstairs. The center hall and main staircase are extremely narrow—charming, but also rather inconvenient. Henry James wrote affectionately about visiting the house in *The American Scene*, but noted "the small, incommodius study" and "the limited library."[3] The interiors today are as Irving left them, preserved in place by a century of adoring descendants, with his desk, books, piano, and flute. The house has been curated since 1945 by Historic Hudson Valley, which operates the site as a public museum.

Lyndhurst

Tarrytown, Westchester County, 1838–65

The Romantic Revival period in the Hudson River began with Sunnyside, the successful, though eccentric, collaboration between gifted amateur architects, Washington Irving and his friend George Harvey. Lyndhurst, originally Knoll because of the topography, and later Lyndenhurst because of the fine linden trees on the site, is a different matter altogether. It is a masterpiece, in a style then new, by a professional architect, Alexander Jackson Davis.

Lyndhurst is the quintessential American Gothic Revival house. When it was built, the great era of the American country house had begun, and the site just north of Sunnyside was prime real estate. In spite of its Gothic seriousness and its almost ecclesiastical attitude, Lyndhurst was built as a weekend and summer house, a rural retreat for New Yorkers escaping to rusticate.

Davis was only thirty-five years old when he received the commission from William Paulding (1770–1854), a New York City lawyer and former mayor, and his son Philip (1816–1864). Davis's newly published *Rural Residences* featured illustrations and plans for several houses in the Gothic taste, including one large complex stone villa "in the English collegiate style," which certainly prefigures his design for the Pauldings. Davis had a background in the fine arts and architectural illustration, and his talents are easily seen in the beautiful watercolor renderings of Knoll from the east and south, now in the Metropolitan Museum of Art.

The climax of Knoll was the medival hall on the second floor, running east-west, and, with its attendant bedroom, held aloft by the rooms and porches below. Designed for the Pauldings' library, the room recalls an English church or timbered hall, and may have been inspired by an illustration in Loudon's *Encyclopedia of Cottage, Farm, and Villa Architecture.*[1] With an immense Gothic-arched window at the western end, complete with stained glass decoration, this room is the central space of the interior and a strong organizational force in the complex massing of the house as a whole.

ABOVE: *The vestibule.*

RIGHT: *The hallway with a long view to the 1865 wing and the dining room.*

PAGES 186–87: *The library on the second floor is now used as a picture gallery.*

In 1865, Davis made many additions to the building for the second owner, George Merritt. Davis very deftly raised the second story roofs and added an extensive north (or "dining room") wing with a second tower. The medieval hall-library remains the principal element of the interior, although the new five-story tower on the northwest corner becomes the dominant exterior element. Since he used the same local limestone that the original house had been faced with, it is impossible to tell that the composition was designed and built in two stages. The somewhat overwhelming, "pointed" effect of the whole building is greatly softened by the balance between the smooth stone wall surface and the intricacies of detail in fenestration and roofline.

At first glance, the house seems forbidding, but in fact, the entry sequence of porte cochere, piazza, glazed vestibule, and entrance hall is all charming in scale and detail. The piazzas that wrap the south and west facades are beautifully crafted of small pieces of wood creating colonettes and vaulted ceilings. Views from these porches back through the many French doors connecting the rooms inside to the outdoors reveal the house as a design for indoor-outdoor living, a delightful place to be in the summer.

Davis was a brilliant furniture designer as well as architect, and he designed approximately 150 pieces of furniture for the house, some for the Pauldings and some for the Merritts. The earlier pieces have a clean and simple Gothic Revival line, but by the 1860s, the designs became very elaborate and more Victorian. Much of this furniture is in place in the house today.

The last private owners of Lyndhurst were Jay Gould and his daughters. Gould, the railroad tycoon, bought the house in 1880. Like many plutocrats of the late nineteenth century, he was a horticultural enthusiast, and he developed a enormous plant collection in the greenhouses the Merritts had built around 1870. Full of Gould's plants, the huge structure, onion dome and all, burned to the ground in 1880. It was immediately rebuilt in 1881, by the famous glasshouse firm Lord and Burnham (conveniently headquartered down the road in Irvington), with Gothic Revival details. The whole greenhouse complex has not been maintained for many years and today awaits restoration.

Lyndhurst was bequeathed to the National Trust for Historic Preservation by Gould's daughter, Anna, Duchess of Talleyrand-Perigord, in 1961. The property still descends to the river's edge. There is no record of Downing having worked at this site, but the magnificent collections of mature deciduous trees—beeches, lindens, maples and oaks—make this one of the finest traditional estate landscapes in America.

Nuits

Irvington, Westchester County, c. 1853–60

Nuits is one of many fine examples of the Romantic Revival in American architecture along the Hudson in the short stretch of the old Albany Post Road from Tarrytown south to Ardsley. In the period from 1835 until the Civil War, a new house in this Irving- and Downing-influenced stretch of the Hudson Valley would almost inevitably be designed as a picturesque cottage or villa, either Gothic Revival or Italianate.

The Italianate Nuits was designed not by a member of the Irving-Downing-Davis circle but by an outsider under their influence, Detlef Lienau (1818–1888), a Danish-born architect trained in Munich and Paris. Arriving in New York in 1848, he established himself very quickly in the early 1850s, becoming for a time the partner of Leon Marcotte, the highly successful architect/decorator. In the design for Nuits, Lienau may have been influenced by the writings of Davis and Downing. Or he might have seen the celebrated Italianate house in Newport, built in 1845 by Richard Upjohn for Edward King and illustrated in 1850 by Downing in his latest statement on style.

Lienau was European, and so was his client, Francis Cottenet (1795–1884), who had come from Nuits-St.-George in France in 1818 and made a fortune importing textiles from Europe. Cottenet, who lived in Manhattan in a lower Fifth Avenue mansion, commissioned Lienau to build Nuits, named after his birthplace, as a summer residence. The house is constructed of brick, but it is faced with Caen stone, a soft limestone that was brought from France as ballast in Cottenet's ships. The stone was shipped to Dobbs Ferry and hauled overland to the site, originally a 14-acre estate on the river. Just next door stood Nevis, the 1835 Greek Revival house of James Alexander Hamilton, son of Alexander Hamilton.[1]

The Caen stone makes Nuits truly remarkable. No other New York Italianate house is built of this luxuriant, creamy material. The landscape design, with the large specimen trees planted at a distance, ensures that the house sits always in the sunshine.

OPPOSITE: *Andrew Jackson Downing's 1850 illustration of the King house in Newport, perhaps a model for Nuits.*

Bathed in the strong sun, the west, or river, facade and the entrance front on the south glow an alluring soft yellow at many times of the day.

Lienau built the house in two stages, the south entrance block in 1853, and the north extension in 1860. Many features of the Italian Renaissance villa as imagined by nineteenth-century picturesque designers are present. A square tower capped by a pyramidal roof rises above the main block. There are deeply overhanging eaves supported by dozens of brackets; an asymmetrical roofline is achieved by many tall sections of the house, sometimes receding and sometimes projecting forward. Canopies and hoods of various designs project over French and bay windows, and a stone arcade with grape-leaf carvings marks the entrance.

The massing of the parts of the building, and the smooth relationships between the parts is strong and elegant. The whole composition is calm in spite of its many elements, sustained by the smooth surface and continuity provided by the light-colored stone. Cornices and brackets and window and door surrounds are painted to match the stone, complementing the soft blue-green of the shutters and selected other elements. The landscaping, the luminous quality of the stone, and the restricted palette all combine to flatter the Italianate design.

Inside, a long hallway extends from the main door to the billiard room in the 1860 extension to the north. There are sixteen sets of French doors, many opening to the piazzas, and the house feels like the summer house it was intended to be. There are

fascinating fireplaces with windows set above their mantelpieces—perhaps a trick Lienau learned in his European training. During the 1860 expansion, a charming conservatory was added by the glasshouse firm Lord and Burnham.

Subsequently owned by industrialist Cyrus Field and John Jacob Astor III and still a private residence, this house recalls Andrew Jackson Downing's romantic pronouncement: "the villa ... should above all things, manifest individuality. It should say something of the character of the family within—as much as possible of ... their tastes and associations, should mold and fashion themselves, upon its walls." He goes on, stating that these are houses for "men of imagination ... men whose ambition and energy will give them no peace.... These are men for picturesque villas."[2]

CHAPTER 7

ECLECTIC STYLES OF THE POST CIVIL WAR PERIOD

The last quarter of the nineteenth century saw the rise of tremendous wealth among the plutocrats and aristocrats of New York, substantial prosperity among the new upper middle class, a new emphasis on leisure and travel around America and back and forth to Europe, the rise of many brilliant and powerful architects, and the emergence of a great variety of architectural styles.

The Hudson River Valley, with all of its legend and romanticism, had become a place where people from New York City, if they could afford it, wanted to spend their weekends and leisure time. Often the wealthiest families, such as the Millses and the Vanderbilts, also had houses at the seashore (Newport or Bar Harbor), where the summer was cooler and more agreeable than it is on the river. But others, such as the artistic set that followed the textile designer Candace Wheeler to her summer colony higher up in the Catskill Mountains, were happy with mountain climbing and botanizing. Up there, high above the river valley, they had altitude on their side.

Some of the new architectural styles were purely American— the stick style, the shingle style, and the Colonial Revival. Others were distinctly un-American—the English Victorian Gothic, the Second Empire, and the Beaux-Arts. An inventive and eclectic architectural firm such as McKim, Mead & White could work in any of these styles. During this period, the grand house designed by a prominent firm attained a new cachet, but there were still many amateurs designing their own houses. Among the many well-known architects of the day, Stanford White, Charles Follen McKim, Calvert Vaux, and Francis L.V. Hoppin were all involved with houses in the Hudson Valley.

Olana, designed not by a firm, but by the artist Frederic Edwin Church, epitomizes the rich and exotic taste of well-traveled and artistic New Yorkers of the late nineteenth-century. The interiors of this splendid house reflect the Aesthetic Movement, seen also in the more modest interiors at Onteora Park. In another vein altogether are the extravagant mansions built by McKim, Mead & White for the Mills and Vanderbilt families as showplaces for clients wanting to be surrounded by European taste, set pieces for high-style living and entertaining.

Springwood is a real family seat—home of Franklin Delano Roosevelt. Perhaps the most publicized of all Hudson River houses, Springwood was rebuilt and expanded in 1915 in an eclectic style, part of which is Colonial Revival, by an architectural firm working closely with an amateur architect and historic preservationist who would be, not many years later, President of the United States.

Armour-Stiner House
Irvington, Westchester County, 1860–72

Orson Squire Fowler's book, A Home for All, or the Gravel Wall and the Octagonal Mode of Building, *spurred a fad for the octagonal house, which Fowler claimed was more efficient and even healthier than other layouts. This house was built in 1860 as a two-story structure, and the simple octagon was expanded upward with a high dome and cupola in the Second Empire style in 1872. Still a private residence, the house is a unique combination of disparate design ideas and elements unified by the ego of the designer and the scale of the dome.*

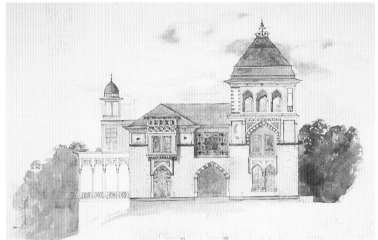

Olana

Hudson, Columbia County, 1870–91

When artists, architects, and writers build houses for their own use, the results are often complex and pace setting. Notable examples in American architecture include Monticello, by Thomas Jefferson, Sunnyside, by Washington Irving, and, of course, the Taliesens of Frank Lloyd Wright. The great American landscape painter Frederic Edwin Church (1826–1900) designed Olana in collaboration with the architect Calvert Vaux, in what he called the "Persian style," which he freely admitted he was inventing. Church had been to the Middle East, although not to Persia in fact, and he was enraptured by Islamic design. Vaux, best known as the designer, with Frederick Law Olmsted, of Central Park, was a romantic architect whose influence is felt at Olana. The details of his partnership with Church are lost, but most scholars credit Church with the spirit of the design and all the decorative details.

Olana the house is set within Olana the designed landscape. The view is among the most celebrated in North America, extending to the southwest, across lawns, woods, and orchards (beauty in the foreground); down to the Hudson River (immensity in the middle ground); across the Wall of Manitou, and up to the peaks of the Catskill Mountains (the sublime in the distance). It is a view Church often painted, and one he sketched when he first visited the site in the mid 1840s with his teacher, Thomas Cole.

Twenty years later, Church began to assemble the property that ultimately became the setting for Olana. In 1867, he acquired the hilltop and began to plan the house, which was designed and built

The entrance facade faces away from the river, but there is a view to the south from the steps.

PAGES 204-5: *The central, cruciform space with its melange of Aesthetic Movement furnishings.*

in two phases. In collaboration with Vaux, the main block was constructed from 1870 to 1872; the studio wing, which Church designed on his own, was built between 1888 and 1891. The house is a massive limestone rubble building with three towers—bell, water, and studio. The original building is richly encrusted with orientalizing ornament—fourteen types of brick in many colors, glazed tiles, applied metalwork, polychrome painting on cornices, teapots used as finials—and roofed with red, blue, and green slate, with occasional gilded slates reflecting the sky. There are ombras and ogive arches, bay windows, projecting balconies and recessed porches. However fantastic, the whole original composition is firmly lodged into the sloping site and has great presence and weight.

Within is a set of designed "Oriental" interiors: gorgeously decorated, theatrical rooms arranged in a cruciform plan around a central court, reminiscent of those Church had seen in the houses of Beirut and Damascus on his trip there with his wife in 1867–69.[1] The rooms are exotic melanges that are stenciled, decorated with carved teak mantels and doorknobs, lit by painted windows ornamented by cut-paper designs, and richly hung with works by old masters and nineteenth-century American artists. Of particular note is the collection of Indian carvings and furniture acquired from Lockwood de Forest, a former student of Church who later formed Associated Artists in partnership with Louis Comfort Tiffany and Candace Wheeler.

Olana is a monument to the Aesthetic Movement, which flourished in America between 1870 and 1900, spurred by the eye-opening exhibition of Japanese art at the Centennial Exhibition of 1876 and the growing taste for exoticism among American painters and writers.[2] In her book on orientalism, Holly Edwards writes of the

At the foot of the stairs is an array of Middle Eastern metalwork and textiles.

OPPOSITE: *Many carved teak elements were provided by the Ahmedabad, India, workshops of Lockwood de Forest.*

"convergence of artistic sensitivity and the lust for travel" among Church and his peers.[3] The tradition extended throughout much of the nineteenth century, embracing both Washington Irving's *Alhambra* (1832) and late-nineteenth-century design ideas such as those expressed by Louis Sullivan in the decorative scheme of the Wainwright building in St. Louis (1890–91).[4]

Working on Olana from 1870 onward, designing polychrome stenciled cornices and borders, decorating windows and interior doors, and blending a wide repertory of designs and materials into a unique whole composition, Church was a leader in the American Aesthetic Movement. Church had long been established as a major figure in American exploration of exoticism in the visual arts—his paintings of the landscape and volcanoes of South America and the icebergs of Newfoundland had made him rich and famous.

American taste was changing in the post-Civil War period, and his work was beginning to be out of fashion.[5] By 1870, Olana, the house and the landscape, had become his primary canvas.

Church lavished time and money on the vast landscape he designed in the picturesque taste. He created a designed 250-acre estate with the original farm fields and orchards, far below Olana, as part of the view from the house. Church also created the lake at the bottom of the hill and planted woods behind it and to the side so that the view downhill and to the east was complex and interesting, complementing, in its nearness, the vastness of the river and Catskills view to the west. Some landscape historians believe this may be the most important nineteenth-century American picturesque landscape still intact. All of Church's original acreage remains with the house today, and a complete restoration is possible.

TOP AND RIGHT: *The studio in the house.*

ABOVE: *Frederic Edwin Church,* Sunset across the Hudson Valley, *1870.*

Cooper-Hewitt, National Design Museum, Smithsonian Institution

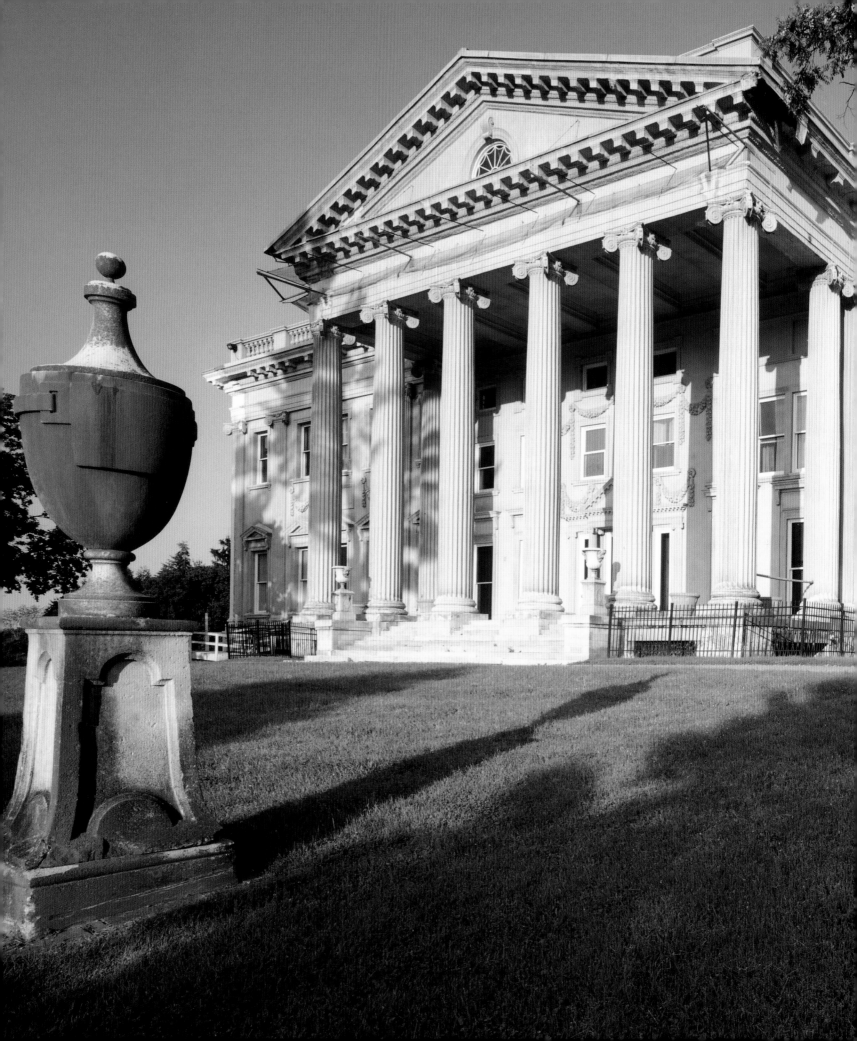

Staatsburgh

Hyde Park, Dutchess County, 1896

Hyde Park:
The Vanderbilt Mansion

Hyde Park, Dutchess County, 1899

Mr. and Mrs. Ogden Mills were late-nineteenth-century American plutocrats with a high position in New York society. The fortune derived from his father's success in the California gold rush of 1849, and the social position was hers— over two hundred years of Livingston forebears. The Millses lived an elegant and fashionable life, and some social historians have felt that Mrs. Mills could have succeeded Mrs. William Backhouse Astor as the leader of New York society except for her infamous superciliousness. As the New York historian Jerry Patterson says, "Mrs. Mills had every qualification except personality."[1]

The Millses were perfect Edith Wharton characters, with vast worldly possessions (a yacht to make sailing up river from New York a pleasure and a Pullman railroad car to make the train trip comfortable) and vast leisure. They staged frequent house parties with many friends staying for days on end, and they loved playing bridge. It is thought that Staatsburgh was the model for the great Hudson River country house Wharton's heroine Lily Bart visits in *The House of Mirth*, where, gambling at cards after dinner with people of great wealth, the modest Lily alarmingly loses much more than she can afford.

In 1890, Mrs. Mills inherited an 1832 Greek Revival mansion, called Staatsburgh, and substantial riverfront property that had been part of her Livingston grandmother's real estate holdings. The Millses, who had been married in 1882, already owned a palatial New York town house by Richard Morris Hunt and, in keeping with their social position and Gilded Age custom, they had other houses in California, Newport, and Paris. The Hudson River house was used for weekends when they were in New York and for a long stay in the late summer (after the Newport season) and fall (until the New York season).

*The dining room, decorated by
Jules Allard et fils of Paris.*

RIGHT: *A portrait of Mrs. Mills hangs
in her French-style morning room.*

The Millses used the original Greek Revival house for a few years before retaining McKim, Mead & White to update, re-fashion, and expand the building in the mid 1890s. The result is an Anglo-American country house of large proportions, and a perfect example of the way very rich and well-traveled Americans wanted to live in the last years of the nineteenth century. McKim, Mead & White, with Stanford White as the partner-in-charge, created for them a new "American Renaissance" country house, with the original Greek Revival house at its core, in the style of a mid-eighteenth-century English mansion full of French furniture. The prototype for the design of the entrance facade may have been the James Hoban–Benjamin Latrobe designs for the White House,[2]

A design by the English architect James Gibbs, whose eighteenth-century houses in this style were the forerunners of Staatsburgh.

but it is more likely that both houses derive from the English Baroque mansions designed by James Gibbs, some of which were illustrated in his 1728 *Book of Architecture*.[3]

The original Greek Revival house can be "sensed," if not exactly seen, in the center section of the expanded building, behind the magnificent Ionic portico. The new flanking wings are articulated on the facades with giant fluted pilasters rising to a massive entablature below a classical balustrade. Originally white stucco, the exterior is severe and grandiose, an effect exacerbated by the immense plate glass, one-over-one sash windows.

In spite of its forbidding scale, the interior of the house is ingenious and rather charming in its eccentricity. White created a huge L-shaped living hall at the entrance, in his own tradition, complete with grand staircase, oak-paneled walls and ceiling, a major fireplace, and floor to ceiling windows opening onto the terrace on the river front. This double-height room occupies much of the volume of the original 1832 house. To the left of the hall, White combined the two original drawing rooms, creating an awkwardly long and narrow space. In the wings are the two new grand rooms of the mansion—the dining room on the north and the library on the south.

To design and decorate these rooms, White retained Jules Allard et fils of Paris. The dining room is hung with a set of four large Flemish tapestries, which have been altered to fit the marble walls, and furnished in late-nineteenth-century reproductions of eighteenth-century French furniture. The library, reached through a long enfilade, is more English in style, with gilt and oak paneling and an agreeable clutter of chairs and desks and family paintings.

Staatsburgh has an exceptionally beautiful setting, looking west across a vast lawn, through the branches of trees at the edge of the river, across the water to the Shawangunk and Catskill Mountains. The river seems to swing around the property, creating

the sense of this being a huge point of land, an illusion created by Mills Cove, a small inlet to the north of the great lawn. In the eighteenth-century English style pioneered by Capability Brown, great clumps of mature deciduous and coniferous trees have been artfully placed to enhance the view from the house, which sits high above the lawn as it descends to the river.

After Mrs. Mills died in 1920, the house was no longer used by the family on a regular basis. It was given to New York State in 1938 by Mrs. Mills's daughter, and is maintained today as it was in 1920.

Hyde Park, the even more magnificent palace of Frederick William Vanderbilt, is the centerpiece of a large estate just to the south of Staatsburgh. It was completed in 1899, also by McKim, Mead & White.

But unlike Staatsburgh, this house was the project of Charles F. McKim, and the taste here is more Italian. The decorating was the work of McKim, Mead & White and Ogden Codman Jr. The Vanderbilt grounds are of great interest because of the romantic landscape garden laid out about 1830 around the earlier house on the property. In the 1830s, André Parmentier, a Belgian landscape designer, was brought to the site by Dr. David Hosack, then New York's most celebrated horticulturist, who owned the house at that time. The fine specimen trees and the picturesque layout are of the Parmentier period, a landscape that was of great interest to Downing and later to the Vanderbilts. The house and grounds were given to the American people by the Vanderbilt family at the suggestion of Franklin D. Roosevelt, and they are operated today as a public museum by the National Park Service.

Minnehaha

Onteora Park, Greene County, c. 1899

The Hudson Valley is broadly defined by mountain ranges to the east and west, creating high walls above the river plain. Far to the east are the Berkshire and Taconic Hills, but the Catskill Mountains, on the west side of the river, are close and they are the most prominent. The eastern peaks of the Catskills and the Escarpment, also known as the Great Wall of Manitou, dramatically define the western limit of the river valley and provide a magnificent distant view for the riverfront houses on the east bank. The Catskills are partners of the Hudson River. Early on, they were called the "Blue Mountains," because when the Escarpment assumes this color on hazy days it is supposed to signify good weather.

A particular brand of American summer architecture grew up in the Catskills in the late nineteenth century, and nowhere is it more clearly seen than in Onteora Park, the first of several summer artists' colonies established after the Civil War. Onteora, near Tannersville, was founded in the 1880s by Candace Wheeler, the New York textile designer, interior designer, and feminist.

Wheeler and her group built their first rustic "camps," or summer houses, in 1883, the very year when railway service reached Tannersville. These were simple but artistic "cottages" for creative professional people and designed for "plain living and high thinking."[1] The first generation of Onteora houses evoked local vernacular farmhouses, but with picturesque elements—low-profile cottages with pitched roofs and dormers, asymmetrical elevations and plans, and many porches replete with twig railings. To capture mountain views, the houses had many windows, usually casements with small rectangular and diamond-shaped lights. Several of these houses were designed by Candace's son, Dunham Wheeler.

The interiors were decorated in a countrified version of the opulent, urban style of the Aesthetic Movement, promoted by Wheeler and her New York City design partners Louis Comfort Tiffany and Lockwood de Forest. Filled with handmade Arts and Crafts furniture, objects in the Japanese and Islamic taste, and

The entrance court. At the top of the
house on the left is a boom that was
used with a pulley system for hoisting
steamer trunks into the attic. This
was a summer house, with guests
frequently coming and going.

OPPOSITE: *The front door.*

The central room with its balcony
and Moroccan lantern.

OPPOSITE: *An American cupboard
full of Russian Easter eggs and
Bohemian glass.*

Persian and Indian rugs, the early houses had great stone fire-places, rooms lined with unpainted flush board paneling, and no plumbing. Wheeler eschewed plumbing and kitchens. As a career woman and a role model, she thought women should not be wasting their time cooking. An Onteora inn with a dining room and a good French chef was an early amenity.

Wheeler and her group lost control of the enclave in the 1890s, and a new generation began buying in. They were not always so high-minded, they were usually richer, and they wanted bigger houses, plumbing, and dinner at home. Candace Wheeler did not approve, and eventually she left Onteora.[2]

Minnehaha is one of the "second generation" houses. It was designed by the Canadian artist and architect George A. Reid, who ultimately built some twenty "cottages" as well as the Onteora

church and library. Three-stories tall, this house is a more self-conscious and professional design than the earlier houses. Minnehaha is a hybrid of the Catskill style developed in the 1880s by the Wheeler group and the shingle style that was so pervasive in East Coast resorts. The continuous use of shingles on the roof and exterior walls, the numerous covered porches, the twig porch railings, the long banks of casement windows, the high gambrel roofline, the huge stone chimneys, the sleeping porches, and the open, flowing, asymmetrical floor plan all combine to make the house Catskill shingle style.

The central living hall is two stories high with a second floor balcony all around and a beamed and wood-paneled ceiling. With a focus on the immense fireplace and exposed stone chimney, this room is surrounded, outside, by an asymmetrical arrangement of porches which face the mountain views, and, inside, by a set of adjacent spaces—a dining room, a library, and an open stair and entrance hall. All of these rooms are smaller with low ceilings to emphasize the drama of the two-story central room. The fluid plan relates to those of Frank Lloyd Wright's Prairie School houses, some of which were being designed at the very moment this house was conceived.

Today Minnehaha is decorated with a highly quirky and eclectic collection of American, French, and Islamic furniture and decorative arts. The big central room is lighted by an immense Moroccan hanging lantern. Candace Wheeler might not have approved of George Reid's big house, but she would be comfortable indeed in this twenty-first century Aesthetic Movement interior.

Springwood: Home of Franklin Delano Roosevelt

Hyde Park, Dutchess County, c. 1826–1915

The Roosevelt family had lived in the Hudson Valley for generations before Franklin Delano Roosevelt was born at Springwood in 1882. The estate was acquired by his father, James R. Roosevelt, in 1866 after the family's first river seat just north of Poughkeepsie was destroyed by fire. The house faces east, toward the road, formerly the King's Highway or Albany Post Road, and it occupies a level, rectangular platform that drops off dramatically to an open meadow on the south, and to woods on the west, with the Hudson below.

Eclectic as it is, Springwood can be most closely associated with the Colonial Revival style introduced in the 1915 renovation by Franklin Delano Roosevelt and his widowed mother, Sara Delano Roosevelt. Working with Roosevelt and his mother was Francis L.V. Hoppin of Hoppin & Koen, a New York firm that designed many country seats including the Andrew C. Zabriskie house up the river at the Blithewood estate at Barrytown and the Mount, Edith Wharton's house in the Berkshires.

The entrance facade is very complicated, a pastiche of several different design ideas. The twin towers have an Italianate feeling, but the center section refers to Charles Bulfinch's Federal architecture of a century earlier in the half round window in the attic, the door and fanlight, the semi-circular porch, the swags and inset decorative panels.[1] The heavy fieldstone wings are another style altogether, although they are of the same date. Designed by FDR himself, they are massive and ponderous, surmounted by a wide and bold entablature and heavy classical balustrades, reminiscent of elements designed by Jefferson at Monticello, and not at all like the Adamesque details of the center section. The most curious thing about the wings is that although they have nearly identical footprints, they are different heights. The south wing accommodating the library is significantly higher and more imposing than the wing on the north, which houses kitchens and other support functions.

These drawings by the Historic American Buildings Survey show the east (or main) elevation and the west (or back) elevation.

RIGHT: *Many elements of the earlier house are visible on the west elevation, including an Italianate porch, probably c. 1840s.*

Springwood's eclectic facade is but a theatrical front applied to two earlier phases of construction. The original house is believed to have been a Federal farmhouse built in 1826, but almost nothing remains from that era. In the late 1840s, the second owner, Josiah Wheeler, renovated the building in the fashionable Italianate or Tuscan Revival style, adding a three-story tower to the south, a kitchen wing on the north, and a long porch or piazza wrapping the east, south, and west elevations. Twenty years later, James R. Roosevelt made many changes, adding new rooms for servants and reconfiguring the entrance hall and staircase. He built the carriage house and other barns and stables for his trotters and thoroughbred horses and determined the general design of the estate grounds.

The interiors are Colonial Revival, although earlier nineteenth-century elements remain in a few rooms. Of the greatest interest is the grand library, realized in an English country-house style. FDR is known to have played an important role in the design, which features mahogany paneling, marble mantels, and views in three directions.[2]

Adjacent to the house is the FDR Library and Museum, sited and designed in the Dutch Colonial style by the President himself in the late 1930s. Roosevelt's hand as a designer pervades the buildings and grounds—in the main house, in the furnishing of his own study

The library in the main house, designed in part by Franklin Delano Roosevelt.

PAGES 236–237: *The hallway, an element of the late 1800s.*

in the Library and Museum, and in Val-kill Cottage, also known as the Stone Cottage, which he designed for Eleanor Roosevelt in the 1920s. In addition, he left specific instructions and dimensions for his own tomb, and sited it in his mother's rose garden.

FDR acquired large tracts of farmland from adjacent estates, and he was an enthusiastic grower of trees. In collaboration with a forestry expert from Syracuse University, FDR planted, it is said, up to half a million trees at Springwood. He was proud of his old-growth woodland along the river, contributing large oaks from these woods to the wartime shipping effort in the 1940s.

We meet at Springwood Roosevelt the amateur architect, gentleman farmer, and historic preservationist. He was active in the

Holland Society of New York and contributed introductions to two important books documenting early Dutch houses, *Dutch Houses in the Hudson River Valley* by Helen Wilkinson Reynolds and *Pre-Revolutionary Dutch Houses and Families in Northern New Jersey and Southern New York* by Rosalie Fellows Bailey. Most significantly, perhaps, his presidential administration created the Historic American Buildings Survey (HABS), an agency dedicated to documenting historic buildings that remains a cornerstone of the preservation movement today. Not since Jefferson had a President of the United States been so committed to architecture and design, and certainly no other President ever wrote so warmly about old houses.

The stable built by the President's father for his trotters and thoroughbred horses.

Afterword

Having now been introduced to this superlative group of historic houses, all within a few hours' drive of New York City, the reader may well ask, "What of the future?" The answer is that in the megalopolis between New York City and Albany, urban sprawl, suburban development, the disappearance of small family farms, and industrialization in river towns all pose serious consequences for the cultural landscape and context in which these houses are set.

There are some success stories. Working with the National Trust for Historic Preservation and Historic Hudson Valley, the Rockefeller family has protected Kykuit and its historic grounds forever. In fact, because of the deep interest and great generosity of the Rockefellers, several other places are well protected inside their original working landscapes, particularly Van Cortlandt Manor, Sunnyside, and Montgomery Place. The National Trust also stewards Lyndhurst and its large historic garden with considerable success.

But outside these estate gates, the Hudson River Valley is, as Thomas Cole might have prophesied, a threatened place. It was officially designated an endangered region by the National Trust in 2000. Within daily commuting distance of New York City, the counties of Putnam, Dutchess, Orange, and Ulster are now among the fastest growing areas in America. For example, Hyde Park was a quaint village fifty years ago; today it is a populous suburb where inappropriate commercial and residential development encroaches on the Roosevelt, Vanderbilt, and Mills houses and sites, undermining their historical significance.

Working to mitigate damage to the environment, our towns, hamlets, and landscapes, not to mention the loss of our cultural history, are a number of conservation and land trust organizations such as Scenic Hudson and the Dutchess County and Columbia Land Conservancies. Scenic Hudson has a long and successful history of PCB clean up in the river itself, farmland protection, and work with riverfront communities to encourage sustainable development, counteract sprawl, and create public access to the River.

Hudson River Heritage, dedicated to the protection of historic architecture and rural landscape, was responsible for the creation of the Hudson River National Historic Landmark District. This 20-mile long, 22,000-acre section of the riverfront incorporates more than 40 riverfront estates, mainly in Dutchess County. The New York Landmarks Conservancy, based in New York City, conducts architectural preservation programs statewide, including its well-known Sacred Sites program, which aims to help congregations safeguard historic religious buildings.

Still other environmental advocacy organizations are fighting industrialization. Friends of Hudson has recently led a strategic campaign to prevent the construction of an over-sized cement plant near the city of Hudson, otherwise notable for its extensive collection of Federal and Greek Revival town houses. The Preservation League of New York State is a statewide preservation organization, working with all of these groups to protect our built and natural heritage, providing technical, architectural, and legal assistance, and influencing public policy.

Like other beautiful areas adjacent to many of the world's great cities in the early twenty-first century, the Hudson River Valley is greatly endangered. The private sector is, for the most part, in charge of the plan of defense. It is to be hoped that the readers of this book will be called to arms.

Kykuit, Pocantico Hills
Westchester County, 1906–1913

The Rockefeller estate takes its name from kykuit, the Dutch word for look-out and the name of the highest point on the property purchased by John D. Rockefeller Sr. in 1893. That site, with sweeping views of the river and the Palisades, became the setting for the house itself and the magnificent gardens that surround it today. Delano & Aldrich first designed the house in 1906, and it was redesigned and completed by William Wells Bosworth in 1913. The interiors, many designed in the English taste by Ogden Codman Jr., reflect the collecting interests of three generations of the Rockefeller family.

Directory of House Museums

Numbers refer to map.

* These museums are not included in the text of the book.

Madam Brett Homestead Museum* 9
50 Nydeck Avenue
Beacon, NY 12509
(845) 831-6533

Boscobel 8
1601 Route 9D
Garrison, NY 10524
(845) 265-3638
www.boscobel.org

The Bronck Museum 25
US Route 9W
Coxsackie, NY 12051
(518) 731-6490
www.gchistory.org/bronck.html

Cedar Grove 26
218 Spring Street
Catskill, NY 12414
(518) 943-7465
www.thomascole.org

Cherry Hill* 24
523 1/2 South Pearl Street
Albany, NY 12202
(518) 343-4791
www.historiccherryhill.org

Clermont 16
One Clermont Avenue
Germantown, NY 12526
(518) 537-4240
www.friendsofclermont.org

David Crawford House, Newburgh

David Crawford House* 31
189 Montgomery Street
Newburgh, New York 12550
(845) 561-2585
www.newburgh-ny.com/crawford_house

John De Wint House 33
Livingston Avenue and Oak Tree Road
Tappan, NY 10983
(914) 359-1359
www.nymasonichall.org/services/
dewint.html

John Ellison House 32
P.O. Box 207
Vails Gate, NY 12584
(845) 561-5498

Gomez Mill House* 30
11 Mill House road
Marlboro, NY 12542
(845) 236-3126
www.gomez.org

Hart-Cluett House 21
57 Second Street
Troy, New York 12180
(518) 272-7232
www.rchsonline.org

Huguenot Street Historical Society* 28
18 Broadhead Avenue
New Paltz, NY 12561
(845) 255-1889
www.hhs-newpaltz.net

Fred J. Johnston Museum, Kingston

Fred J. Johnston Museum* 27
63 Main Street
Kingston, NY 12401
(845) 339-0720
www.cr.nps.gov/nr/travel/kingston/
k9.htm

Kykuit* 6
Route 9
Sleepy Hollow, NY 10591
(914) 631-3992
www.hudsonvalley.org/web/
kyku-main.html

Locust Grove* 10
Samuel F. B. Morse Historic Site
2683 South Road
Poughkeepsie, NY 12601
(845) 454-4500
www.morsehistoricsite.org

Locust Lawn 29
18 Broadhead Avenue
New Paltz, NY 12561
(845) 255-1660
www.hhs-newpaltz.net

Lyndhurst 4
635 South Broadway
Tarrytown, NY 10591
(914) 631-4481
www.lyndhurst.org

Montgomery Place 15
P.O. Box 32
Annandale-on-Hudson, NY 12504
(845) 758-5264
www.hudsonriverheritage.org/
montgo.html

Olana 17
5270 Route 9G
Hudson, NY 12534
(518) 828-0135
www.olana.org

Philipsburg Manor* 5
341 North Broadway
Sleepy Hollow, NY 10591
(914) 631-3992
www.hudsonvalley.org/web/
phil-main.html

Philipse Manor Hall 2
Warburton Avenue and Dock Street
PO Box 496
Yonkers, NY 10702
(914) 965-4027
www.philipsemanorfriends.org

Schuyler Mansion 23
32 Catherine Street
Albany, NY 12202
(518) 434-0834

Springwood: FDR Historical Site 11
4097 Albany Post Road
Hyde Park, NY 12538
(845) 229-0021
www.nps.gov/hofr/

Staatsburgh 13
PO Box 308
Old Post Road
Staatsburg, NY 12580
(845) 889-8851
www.staatsburgh.org

Sunnyside 3
West Sunnyside Lane
Tarrytown, NY 10591
(914) 631-8200
www.hudsonvalley.org/web/
sunn-main.html

Ten Broeck Mansion 22
9 Ten Broeck Place
Albany, NY 12210
(518) 436-9826
www.tenbroeck.org

Luykas Van Alen House 18
Route 9H
Kinderhook, NY 12106
(518) 758-9265
www.cchsny.org/prog_links_sites_1.html

Martin Van Buren National Historic Site* 19
Lindenwald
1013 Old Post Road
Kinderhook, NY 12106
(518) 758-9689
www.nps.gov/mava/

Vanderbilt Mansion National Historic Site 12
4097 Albany Post Road
Hyde Park, NY 12538
(845) 229-9115
www.nps.gov/vama/home.htm

Van Cortlandt Manor 7
525 South Riverside Avenue
Croton-on-Hudson, NY 10520
(914) 271-8981
www.hudsonvalley.org/web/
vanc-main.html

Frederick Van Cortlandt House 1
Broadway at West 246th Street
Bronx, NY 10471
(718) 543-3344
www.vancortlandthouse.org

James Vanderpoel House 20
Route 9
Kinderhook, NY 12106
(518) 758-9265
www.cchsny.org/prog_links_sites_1.html

Wilderstein* 14
PO Box 383
Rhinebeck, NY 12572
(845) 876-4818
www.wilderstein.org

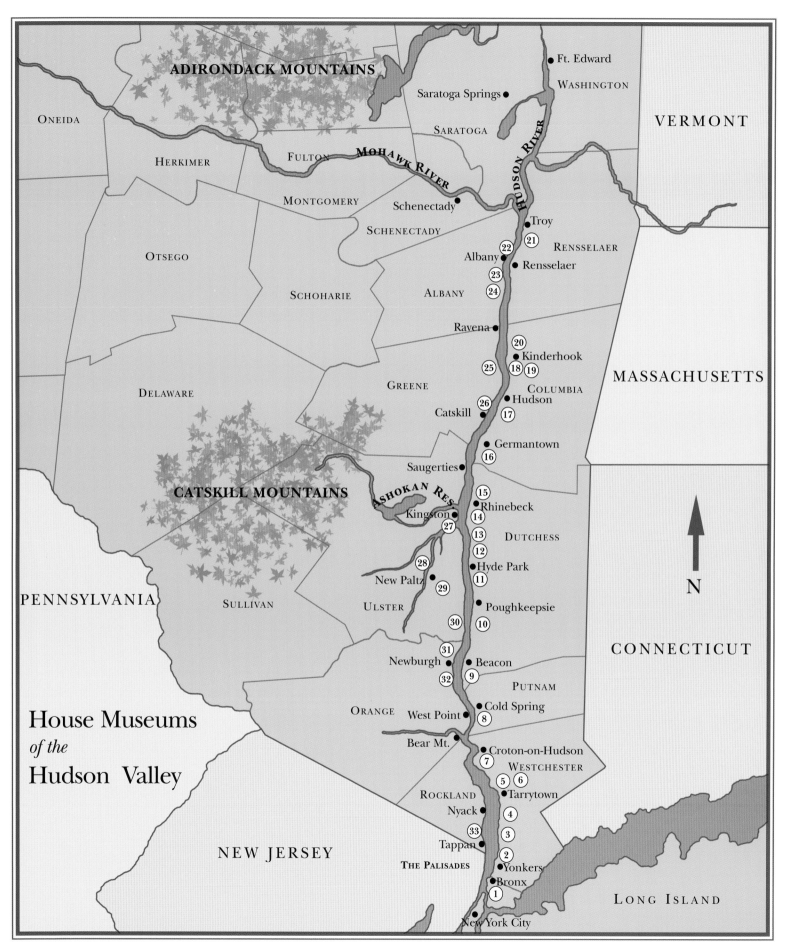

House Museums
of the
Hudson Valley

ADIRONDACK MOUNTAINS

ONEIDA

HERKIMER

FULTON

MONTGOMERY

SCHENECTADY

Schenectady

SCHOHARIE

OTSEGO

DELAWARE

CATSKILL MOUNTAINS

Kingston

PENNSYLVANIA

SULLIVAN

ULSTER

New Paltz

ORANGE

West Point

Bear Mt.

ROCKLAND

Nyack

Tappan

NEW JERSEY

THE PALISADES

New York City

Ft. Edward

WASHINGTON

Saratoga Springs

SARATOGA

MOHAWK RIVER

HUDSON RIVER

Troy

Albany

Rensselaer

RENSSELAER

ALBANY

Ravena

Kinderhook

COLUMBIA

Hudson

Catskill

Germantown

Saugerties

ASHOKAN RES.

Rhinebeck

DUTCHESS

Hyde Park

Poughkeepsie

Newburgh

Beacon

PUTNAM

Cold Spring

Croton-on-Hudson

WESTCHESTER

Tarrytown

GREENE

VERMONT

MASSACHUSETTS

CONNECTICUT

N

LONG ISLAND

Time Line:
Hudson Valley Architecture in Context

1609	Henry Hudson sails up the Hudson and names it "North River"
	Dutch control established
1629	Dutch West India Company establishes patroonships
1629	Patroonship of Rensselaerswyck granted to Killian Van Rensselaer
1647-64	Administration of Peter Stuyvesant
1663–1738	**The Bronck Houses**
1664	The Dutch surrender, and British control of New York established
1677	New Paltz patent granted to 12 French Huguenot families
c. 1682–1755	**Philipse Manor Hall**
1686	Livingston Manor granted to Robert Livingston
1697	"Great Nine Partners' Patent" established in Dutchess County
1700	**John DeWint House**
1710	Pieter Schuyler, the first Mayor of Albany, takes four Iroquois chieftains to London to meet Queen Anne
1737	**Luykas Van Alen House**
1748	**Van Cortlandt Manor House**
	Frederick Van Cortlandt House
1754	**John Ellison House**
1755–61	French and Indian War
c. 1758–60	**Lithgow**
1761	**Schuyler Mansion**
c. 1767–1772	**Wynkoop House**
1776	American Independence declared
1776	British invade New York City
1777	Surrender of Burgoyne after the Battle of Saratoga or Bemis Heights
1777	Kingston made capital of New York
1777	Burning of Kingston by the British
1777	New York's constitutional government established and George Clinton elected Governor for the first of his seven terms
1778–1893	**Clermont** (rebuilding and alteration)
1782	Final winter encampment of the Continental Army, at New Windsor
1783	British evacuation of New York City
1783	Treaty of Paris ends War of Independence
1784	Establishment of City of Hudson by New England whaling families
1785	**Henry I. Van Rensselaer House**
1789	Establishment of City of Troy
1790–1820	New York's population nearly quadrupled
c. 1795–1840	**Silvernail Homestead**
1798	**Ten Broeck Mansion**
1799	Bill passed legalizing gradual emancipation of slaves
1800	Thomas Jefferson elected President
1803	Louisiana Purchase
1804	Death of Alexander Hamilton
1804–5	**Montgomery Place**
1804–8	**Boscobel**
c. 1805	**Jacob Rutsen Van Rensselaer House**
1807	Robert Fulton's first steamboat journey
1812–14	War with Great Britian
c. 1814	**Locust Lawn**
1815–1915	A period when New York Harbor handled over half of all U.S. imports
1815	**Cedar Grove**
c. 1815	**Eastview**
c. 1819	**Vanderpoel House**
1825	Opening of the Erie Canal
c. 1825	Edgewater
1827	**Hart–Cluett House**
	Last slaves in New York freed
1828	Andrew Jackson elected President
1835–1847	**Sunnyside**
1838–65	**Lyndhurst**
1839	Death of the last Patroon of Rensselaerwyck
c. 1840	**Oakcliff**
	Samuel Huntting House
1844	**Henry Delamater House**
1846	Manorial system ended by state Constitutional Convention
1850	Missouri Compromise
1851	Completion of Hudson River Railroad
1852	Death of Andrew Jackson Downing by drowning in the Hudson
1853–60	**Nuits**
1860–72	**Armour-Stiner House**
1861	Civil War begins at Charleston
1865	Lee's surrender at Appomattox
1896	**Staatsburgh**
1870–91	**Olana**
1893	World's Columbian Exposition, Chicago
1899	**Hyde Park: The Vanderbilt Mansion**
c. 1899	**Minnehaha**
1906–13	**Kykuit**
1915	**Springwood**
1917	America enters World War I

Notes

I am immensely grateful to all of the owners of the private houses and the curators of the house museums in this book for teaching me so much. And I am equally grateful to all of the authors and experts cited below, without whose scholarship and guidance a book like this could never be written. G.L.

Introduction

1. Henry James, "New York and the Hudson: A Spring Impression," *The American Scene* (1907; reprint, New York: Penguin Books, 1994): 116.

The Bronck Museum

1. Mendel. Mesick. Cohen. Waite. Architects, The Bronck House Historic Structure Report (unpublished, 1981): 9.

2. Some members of the curatorial staff of the Greene County Historical Society do not agree with the conclusion put forth in the Historic Structure Report, pages 21 and 22. They believe that the wing's construction is so similar to that of the original 1663 building that it must have followed closely on the early building and preceded the brick wing of 1738.

John DeWint House

1. Wilfred Blanch Talman, *Tappan: 300 Years, 1689–1986* (Tappan, New York: The Tappantown Historical Society, 1988): 5. "Slote" is Dutch for "ditch."

2. Rosalie Fellows Bailey, *Pre-Revolutionary Dutch Houses and Families in Northern New Jersey and Southern New York* (New York: William Morrow & Company, 1936): 175.

3. Ibid.: 191.

4. Ibid.

Philipse Manor Hall

1. For a thorough discussion of the English and European Dutch architectural traditions which led to mid-eighteenth-century American houses such as this, see Ruth Selden's unpublished manuscript, *Architectural History of Philipse Manor Hall* (1976), available at Philipse Manor Hall.

2. For more on Hardcastle, see Luke Beckerdite, ed., "Origins of the Rococo Style in New York Furniture and Interior Architecture" in *American Furniture* (1993).

Frederick Van Cortlandt House

1. I am grateful to Laura Correa, Director of the Frederick Van Cortlandt House, for this information.

John Ellison House

1. Hugh Goodman, "The Stone Houses of William Bull," *Orange County Historical Society Journal* 20, 1 (1991): 39.

2. For a good discussion on the evolution of classical houses, see Daniel D. Reiff, *Houses from Books: Treatises, Pattern Books, and Catalogs in American Architecture, 1738–1950: A History and Guide* (University Park, Pennsylvania: The Pennsylvania State University Press, 2000): 11–19.

3. Ibid.: 27.

Lithgow

1. Helen Wilkinson Reynolds, *Dutchess County Doorways, and Other Examples of Period Work in Wood, 1730–1830* (New York: William Farquhar Payson, 1931): 134.

2. Milton M. Klein, ed., *The Empire State: A History of New York* (Ithaca, New York: Cornell University Press, 2001): 154.

3. I am grateful to Dr. Michael Balick and Dr. Kim Tripp of The New York Botanical Garden for this information.

Wynkoop House

1. Nathaniel Lloyd, *A History of the English House* (London: The Architectural Press, 1931): 118. Lloyd writes that moveable sash windows operated by counter-weight and pulley systems were established in English buildings by the late seventeenth century.

2. New York State Department of Parks and Recreation, Schuyler Mansion: A Historic Structure Report (unpublished, 1977): 21. London crown window glass was a process of making sheet glass by hand until around 1800.

3. Gary X. Tinterow, Cornelius Wynkoop House: National Register of Historic Places Application, 5.

Schuyler Mansion

1. See Anna K. Cunningham, *Schuyler Mansion: A Critical Catalogue of the Furnishings and Decorations* (Albany: New York State Education Department, 1955): 6. See also, for a full discussion of the architecture and decoration of the house, Schuyler Mansion: A Historic Structure Report: 12–26. Much of the information in the following section is from this report.

2. Historic Structure Report.: 66. This report also reveals that in 1798 Schuyler himself made a detailed inventory of his window sash and the glass in his windows, of which he was obviously very proud. Period documents such as this have guided the restoration of the building.

Clermont

1. Bruce E. Naramore, *A Driving Tour of Livingston Manor* (The Friends of Clermont, Inc. n.d.): 1.

2. French taste pervaded the Livingston houses at this period. Chancellor Livingston built a new house near his mother's in 1793. It was known as New Clermont or Arryl House. This house burned to the ground in 1909, but we know it today from various drawings and photographs. It was a Federal house in the new French taste with courtyards and terraces, and a glass conservatory extending the whole length of the south facade. More is to be learned about French taste among the Hudson River aristocracy by reading the entries in this book on Montgomery Place, the Jacob Rutsen Van Rensselaer house, Eastview, and Edgewater.

3. Alf Evers, *The Catskills: From Wilderness to Woodstock* (Garden City, New York: Doubleday & Company, Inc., 1972): 290.

Ten Broeck Mansion

1. Mendel-Mesick-Cohen-Architects, The Ten Broeck Mansion: A Historic Structure Report (unpublished, 1975): 23, note 19. This report is the source of much good information on the Ten Broeck Mansion.

Montgomery Place

1. McKelden Smith, ed., *The Great Estates Region of the Hudson River Valley* (Historic Hudson Valley Press, 1988): 5.

2. Roger G. Kennedy, *Orders from France: The Americans and The French in a Revolutionary World, 1780-1820* (Philadelphia: University of Pennsylvania Press, 1990): 35.

3. "Montgomery Place Mansion" in *Historic American Buildings Survey Notes*, Part 1, Item No. 6: 4.

4. The American craze for all things Italian was well underway by this date. For example, Nathaniel Hawthorne's Italian novel *The Marble Faun* was published in 1860.

5. Quoted in Jacquetta M. Haley, *Pleasure Grounds, Andrew Jackson Downing and Montgomery Place* (Tarrytown, New York: Sleepy Hollow Press, 1988): 44.

Boscobel

1. The design of the loggia makes reference to Plate 56 in Book II of Palladio's *I Quattro Libri*.

2. The Pain connection was discussed by Berry B. Tracy in lectures he delivered on May 23 and 24, 1977, notes from which are included in *Docent Training Manual for Boscobel Restoration* (1997). The William Pain publication cited by Tracy was *The Gentleman and Country Builder's Companion* (London, 1794).

3. Harold Kirker, *The Architecture of Charles Bulfinch* (Cambridge, MA: Harvard University Press, 1969): 42–43.

4. Mills B. Lane, *Architecture of the Old South: Maryland* (New York: Abbeville Press, 1991): 66.

5. This observation was made by Charles T. Lyle, executive director of Boscobel Restoration, Inc., in a 2003 conversation with the author.

6. This is according to Frederick Stanyer, then executive director of Boscobel, quoted in Frank Donegan, "Boscobel on the Hudson," *Americana* (December 1991).

Jacob Rutsen Van Rensselaer House

1. Roger G. Kennedy, *Orders from France*: 62–70.

Cedar Grove: The Thomas Cole National Historic Site

1. Ellwood C. Parry, III, "On the Outsider Looking In: Thomas Cole as a Critic of American Culture," in *Thomas Cole: Drawn to Nature* (Albany: Albany Institute of History and Art, 1993): 35. Much of what I have learned about Cole comes from Parry's major biography *The Art of Thomas Cole: Ambition and Imagination* (Newark: University of Delaware Press, 1988).

Eastview

1. Harold Kirker, *The Architecture of Charles Bulfinch*: 128–34.

James Vanderpoel House

1. Paul Wilstach, *Hudson River Landings* (New York: Tudor Publishing Co., 1937): 282.

2. David Maldwyn Ellis, *New York: State and City* (Ithaca and London: Cornell University Press, 1979): 125.

Edgewater

1. William H. Pierson Jr., *American Buildings and Their Architects: The Colonial and Neo-Classical Styles* (Garden City, NY: Anchor Press/Doubleday, 1976): 295.

2. These Federal period, Roman Revival temple fronts, perhaps all inspired by Jefferson, were not the earliest pre-Greek Revival temple fronts, of course. Inspired not by ancient Roman architecture, but by the Italian Renaissance designs of Andrea Palladio, English house designs included temple fronts all through the eighteenth century, and one New York City house still standing today, the Morris-Jumel Mansion in upper Manhattan, has a portico probably dating from the 1780s. The Browns might have been to England, and they certainly had been to Manhattan so these Palladian buildings might also have been their models.

3. Michael Middleton Dwyer, ed., *Great Houses of the Hudson River* (Boston: Little Brown and Company, 2001): 79.

Hart-Cluett House

1. Walter Richard Wheeler, "59 Second Street: Its Design and Construction" in John G. Waite Associates, Architects, PLLC, *The Marble House in Second Street: Biography of A Town House and Its Occupants, 1825-2000* (Troy: Rensselaer County Historical Society, 2000): 85. Much of the information in this chapter comes from this historic structure report, which is a fine model for all other such reports. There are essays by Wheeler, Douglas D. Bucher, and Stacey Pomeroy Draper.

2. Ibid.: 75–79.

Silvernail Homestead

1. Ruth Piwonka and Roderic H. Blackburn, *A Visible Heritage: Columbia County, New York: A History in Art and Architecture* (Kinderhook, New York: The Columbia County Historical Society, 1977): 28.

2. Good information on the family may be found in an unattributed manuscript on Silvernail genealogy on file at the Columbia County Historical Society. The old maps are in the possession of the current owner of the Silvernail house.

3. William H. Pierson Jr. *American Buildings and Their Architects: The Colonial and Neo-Classical Styles*: 214.

Samuel Huntting House

1. All of this information on Nathaniel Lockwood Jr. was found in the Lockwood file at the Dutchess County Historical Society, created by Stephanie Mauri and the late Rosemary O'Mara. I am also grateful to architects John Kinnear and Stephan Falatko for their unpublished research on Dutchess County architecture.

2. Talbot Hamlin, *Greek Revival Architecture in America: Being an Account of Important Trends in American Architecture and American Life prior to the War Between the States* (London: Oxford University Press, 1944): 3.

Picturesque Revival Styles Native to the Hudson Valley

1. Andrew Jackson Downing, *The Architecture of Country Houses* (1850; reprint, New York: Dover Publications, Inc., 1969): 28.

Sunnyside

1. Andrew Jackson Downing, *Landscape Gardening and Rural Architecture* [originally published as *Treatise on the Theory and Practice of Landscape Gardening and Rural Architecture*] (1865; reprint, New York: Dover Publications, Inc., 1991): 354.

2. Alf Evers, *The Catskills: From Wilderness to Woodstock* (Garden City, New York: Doubleday & Company, Inc., 1972): 288–89.

3. Henry James, "New York and the Hudson: A Spring Impression," *The American Scene*: 117.

Lyndhurst

1. Amelia Peck, *Lyndhurst: A Guide to the House and Landscape* (Tarrytown, New York: Lyndhurst, 1988): 28. Peck's writings on Lyndhurst and Davis are classics in the field.

Nuits

1. For much information on Cottenet and Lienau, I am indebted to Louise B. Risk, *Houses on the Hudson* (Privately published, 1993).

2. Andrew Jackson Downing, *The Architecture of Country Houses* (New York: D. Appleton and Company, 1850): 262–63.

Olana

1. James Anthony Ryan, *Frederic Church's Olana: Architecture and Landscape as Art* (Hensonville, New York: Black Dome, 2001): 27. Ryan's book is currently the definitive work on Olana. I am indebted to it for many facts and ideas.

2. Roger B. Stein, "Artifact or Ideology: The Aesthetic Movement in Its American Cultural Context," in *In Pursuit of Beauty: Americans and the Aesthetic Movement* (New York: Metropolitan Museum of Art, 1986): 25.

3. Holly Edwards, et al. *Noble Dreams, Wicked Pleasures: Orientalism in America, 1870–1930* (Willamstown, MA: Princeton University Press and Sterling and Francine Clark Art Institute, 2000): 25.

4. Oleg Grabar, "Roots and Others," in Edwards: 6.

5. John K. Howat, et al, *American Paradise: The World of the Hudson River School* (New York: Metropolitan Museum of Art, 1987): 265.

Staatsburgh

1. Jerry E. Patterson, *The First Four Hundred* (New York: Rizzoli International Publications, 2000): 198.

2. Samuel G. White, *The Houses of McKim, Mead & White* (New York: Rizzoli International Publications, 1998): 177.

3. Pierson, *American Buildings and Their Architects: The Colonial and Neo-Classical Styles*: 399.

Minnehaha

1. Elizabeth Bisland, "A Nineteenth-Century Arcady," *Cosmopolitan* 7 (September, 1889): 519.

2. Amelia Peck and Carol Irish, *Candace Wheeler: The Art and Enterprise of American Design, 1875–1900* (New York: Metropolitan Museum of Art, 1988). For much of what I have learned about Candace Wheeler, I am indebted to this exhibition catalogue.

Springwood

1. See Charles Bulfinch's drawings of the Bingham house, Philadelphia, and the first Harrison Gray Otis House, 1795–96, illustrated in Kirker: 121.

2. Franklin D. Mares, *Springwood* (Roosevelt-Vanderbilt Historical Association, n.d.): 10.

Bibliography

A survey such as this cannot be attempted without all of the deep scholarly work that precedes it. And as the reader learns in these pages, many of these houses could not have been designed or built without the architectural treatises and handbooks that inspired and informed the owners and builders. The most significant books, period and modern, for understanding Hudson River Valley domestic architecture are included below. I acknowledge a great debt to the designers and scholars who have created these key documents.

Arch, Bernd Foerester M. *Architecture Worth Saving in Rensselaer County, New York.* Troy, NY: Rensselaer Polytechnic Institute, 1965.

Bailey, Rosalie Fellows. *Pre-Revolutionary Dutch Houses and Families in Northern New Jersey and Southern New York.* New York: William Morrow & Company, 1936.

Baum, Dwight James, ed., et al. *Great Georgian Houses of America.* Two vols. New York: Kalkhoff Press, 1933–1937. Reprint. New York: Dover Publications, Inc.,1970.

Beckerdite, Luke, ed. "Origins of the Rococo Style of New York Furniture and Interior Architecture," in *American Furniture* (1993).

Benepe, Barry. *Early Architecture in Ulster County.* Kingston, NY: Junior League of Kingston, 1974.

Benjamin, Asher. *The American Builders Companion: or, A System of Architecture Particularly Adapted to the Present Style of Building.* Boston: R. P. C. Williams, 1827. Reprint. New York: Dover Publications, Inc., 1969.

———. *The Country Builder's Assistant.* Greenfield, MA: 1797.

Bennett, Allison P. *The People's Choice: A History of Albany County in Art and Architecture.* Fleischmanns, NY: Purple Mountain Press, 1980.

Bisland, Elizabeth. "A Nineteenth-Century Arcady." *Cosmopolitan* 7. (September 1889).

Blackburn, Roderic H. *Cherry Hill: The History and Collections of a Van Rensselaer Family.* Bethlehem, NY: Historic Cherry Hill, 1976.

Blackburn, Roderic H. and Ruth Piwonka, *Remembrance of Patria: Dutch Arts and Culture in Colonial America, 1609–1776.* Albany, NY: Albany Institute of History and Art, 1988.

Boscobel Restoration, Inc. Docent Training Manual for Boscobel Restoration. 1997.

Boyle, Robert H. *The Hudson River: A Natural and Unnatural History.* New York: W.W. Norton & Company, Inc., 1979.

Carmer, Carl. *The Hudson.* New York and Toronto: Farrar & Rinehart, 1939.

Collier, Edward A. *A History of Old Kinderhook.* New York and London: G.P. Putnam's Sons, 1914.

Cunningham, Anna K. *Schuyler Mansion: A Critical Catalogue of the Furnishings and Decorations.* Albany, NY: New York Department of Education, 1955.

Davis, Alexander Jackson, et al. *Rural Residences.* New York: New York University, 1837. Reprint. New York: DaCapo Press, 1980.

Davidson, Marshall B. *New York: A Pictorial History.* New York: Charles Scribner's Sons, 1977.

Donegan, Frank. "Boscobel on the Hudson." *Americana* (December 1991).

Downing, Andrew Jackson. *The Architecture of Country Houses.* New York: Appleton & Co., 1850. Reprint. New York: Dover Publications, Inc., 1969.

———. *Cottage Residences.* New York: Wiley and Putnam, 1842.

———. *Landscape Gardening and Rural Architecture.* [originally published as *Treatise on the Theory and Practice of Landscape Gardening and Rural Architecture*] New York: Orange Judd Agricultural Book Publisher, 1865. Reprint. New York: Dover Publications, Inc., 1991.

Dunn, Shirley W., and Allison P. Bennett. *Dutch Architecture Near Albany: The Polgreen Photographs.* Fleischmanns, NY: Purple Mountain Press, Ltd., 1996.

Dwyer, Michael Middleton, ed. *Great Houses of the Hudson River.* Boston: Little, Brown and Company, 2001.

Early Marbletown Houses: A Tour Sponsored by Ulster County Historical Society. Kingston, NY: Ulster County Historical Society, 2001.

Eberlein, Harold Donaldson. *The Manors and Historic Houses of the Hudson Valley.* Philadelphia: J.B. Lippincott Company, 1924.

Eberlein, Harold Donaldson, and Cortlandt Van Dyke Hubbard. *Historic Houses of the Hudson Valley.* New York: Architectural Book Publishing Company, Inc. 1942.

Edwards, Holly, with Brian T. Allen, Steven C. Caton, Zeynep Çelik, and Oleg Grabar. *Noble Dreams, Wicked Pleasures: Orientalism in America, 1870–1930.* Williamstown, Massachusetts: Princeton Univeristy Press and Sterling and Francine Clark Art Institute, 2000.

Ellis, David Maldwyn. *Landlords and Farmers in the Hudson-Mohawk Region: 1790–1850.* Ithaca, NY: Cornell University Press, 1946.

———. *New York: State and City.* Ithaca and London: Cornell University Press, 1979.

Ellis, David M., et al. *A History of New York State.* Ithaca, NY: Cornell University Press, 1967.

Evers, Alf. *Catskills: From Wilderness to Woodstock.* Garden City, NY: Doubleday & Company, Inc., 1972.

———. *In Catskill Country: Collected Essay on Mountain History, Life and Lore.* Woodstock, NY: The Overlook Press, 1995.

Fitchen, John. *The New World Dutch Barn: A Study of Its Characteristics, Its Structural System, and Its Probable Erectional Procedures.* Syracuse, NY: Syracuse University Press, 1968.

Flexner, James. *States Dyckman: American Loyalist.* New York: Fordham University Press, 1992.

Groft, Tammis K., and Mary Alice Mackay, eds. *Albany Institute of History and Art: 200 Years of Collecting.* New York: Hudson Hills Press, 1998.

Goodman, Hugh. "The Stone Houses of William Bull." *Orange County Historical Society Journal* 20, 1 (1991).

Gross, Geoffrey, Susan Piatt, and Roderic H. Blackburn. *Dutch Colonial Homes in America.* New York: Rizzoli International Publications, 2002.

Haley, Jacquetta M., ed. *Pleasure Grounds: Andrew Jackson Downing and Montgomery Place.* Tarrytown, NY: Sleepy Hollow Press, 1988.

Hall, Edward Hagaman. *Philipse Manor Hall at Yonkers, N.Y.* New York: The American Scenic and Historic Preservation Society, 1912.

Hamlin, Talbot. *Greek Revival Architecture in America: Being an Account of Important Trends in American Architecture and American Life Prior to the War Between the States.* London: Oxford University Press, 1944.

Heckscher, Morrison H. *Amercian Rococo, 1750–1775: Elegance in Ornament.* New York: Metropolitan Museum of Art, 1992.

Hislop, Codman. *Albany: Dutch, English and American.* Albany, NY: The Argus Press, 1936.

Historic American Buildings Survey, National Park Survey, Department of the Interior. *Montgomery Place Mansion* (HABS No. NY-5625). Washington, D.C., n.d.

History of Columbia County, New York: Illustrations and Biographical Sketches. Philadelphia: J.B. Lippincott & Co., 1878.

Hitchcock, Henry-Russell. *American Architecture Books.* Minneapolis: University of Minnesota Press, 1962.

Howat, John K. *The Hudson River and Its Painters.* New York: The Viking Press, Inc., 1972.

Howat, John K., et al. *American Paradise: The World of the Hudson River School.* New York: The Metropolitan Museum of Art, 1987.

James, Henry. *The American Scene.* New York: Harper and Brothers, 1907. Reprint. New York: Penguin Books, 1994.

John G. Waite Associates, Architects, PLLC. *The Marble House in Second Street: Biography of A Town House and Its Occupants, 1825–2000.* With essays by Douglas G. Bucher, Stacy Pomeroy Draper, and Walter Richard Wheeler. Troy, NY: Rensselaer County Historical Society, 2000.

John Meads (1777–1859): An Albany Cabinetmaker Furnishes Hyde Hall. Springfield, NY: Hyde Hall, 1989.

Johnson, Kathleen Eagen. *The Limner's Trade: Selected Colonial and Federal Paintings from the Collection of Historic Hudson Valley.* North Tarrytown, NY: Philipsburg Manor Gallery, 1996.

Keller, Allan. *Life Along the Hudson.* Tarrytown, NY: Sleepy Hollow Restorations, Inc., 1976.

Kennedy, Roger G. *Greek Revival America.* New York: Stewart, Tabori & Chang, Inc., 1989.

———. *Orders from France: The Americans and The French in a Revolutionary World, 1780–1820.* Philadelphia: University of Pennsylvania Press, 1990.

Kimball, Fiske. *Domestic Architecture of the American Colonies and of the Early Republic.* New York: Charles Scribner's Sons, 1922.

Kirker, Harold. *The Architecture of Charles Bulfinch.* Cambridge, MA: Harvard University Press, 1969.

Klein, Milton M., ed. *The Empire State: A History of New York.* Ithaca, NY: Cornell University Press, 2001.

Lafever, Minard. *The Modern Builder's Guide*. New York: Henry C. Sleight; Collins & Hannay, 1833. Reprint. New York: Dover Publictaions, 1969.

Landy, Jacob. *The Architecture of Minard Lafever*. New York and London: Columbia University Press, 1970.

Lane, Mills B. *Architecture of the Old South: Maryland*. New York: Abbeville Press, 1991.

Lloyd, Nathaniel. *A History of the English House*. London: The Architectural Press, 1931.

Loudon, John Claudius. *The Encyclopedia of Cottage, Farm, and Villa Architecture*. London: Longman, Brown, Green, and Longmans, 1833–42.

Lossing, Benson J. *The Hudson: From the Wilderness to the Sea*. Hensonville, NY: Black Dome Press Corp., 2000.

Major, Howard. *The Domestic Architecture of the Early American Republic*. Philadelphia and London: J.B. Lippincott Company, 1926.

Mares, Franklin D. *Springwood*. Hyde Park, New York: Roosevelt-Vanderbilt Historical Association, n.d.

McEneny, John J. *Albany: Capital City of the Hudson*. New York: Winsdor Publications, 1981.

Meeske, Harrison. *The Hudson Valley Dutch and Their Houses*. Fleischmanns, NY: Purple Mountain Press, Ltd., 1998.

Mendel, Mesick, Cohen Architects. The Ten Broeck Mansion: A Historic Structure Report. Albany, New York: The Albany County Historical Association, 1975.

Mendel. Mesick. Cohen. Waite. Architects. The Bronck House Historic Structure Report. Albany, 1981.

Mesick-Cohen-Waite Architects. The James Vanderpoel House: A Finishes and Furnshings Study. Albany, 1993.

Mesick-Cohen-Waite Architects. The James Vanderpoel House: Historic Structure Report. Albany, 1989.

Millar, Donald. *Measured Drawings of Some Colonial and Georgian Houses*. New York: Architectural Book Publishing Company, Inc., 1915.

Morrison, Hugh. *Early American Architeture From the First Colonial Settlements to the National Period*. New York: Oxford University Press, 1952.

Myers, Kenneth. *The Catskills: Painters, Writers, and Tourists in the Mountains, 1820–1895*. Yonkers, NY: The Hudson River Museum of Westchester, Inc., 1988.

Naramore, Bruce E. *A Driving Tour of Livingston Manor*. The Friends of Clermont, Inc. in cooperation with Clermont State Historic Site, n.d.

Newton, Roger Hale. *Town and Davis Architects, Pioneers in American Revivalist Architecture 1812–1870*. New York: Columbia University Press, 1942.

New York: A Guide to the Empire State. New York: Oxford University Press, 1940.

New York State Department of Parks and Recreation, Division for Historic Preservation. Schuyler Mansion: A Historic Structure Report. Albany, New York, 1977.

Noble, Louis Legrand. *The Life and Works of Thomas Cole*. Hensonville, NY: Black Dome Press Corp., 1997.

Novak, Barbara. *American Painting of the Nineteenth Century: Realism, Idealism, and the American Experience*. New York: Harper & Row, Publishers, 1969.

———. *Nature and Culture: American Landscape and Painting, 1825–1875*. New York and Toronto: Oxford University Press, 1980.

Pain, William. *The Practical Builder*. Boston: 1792.

Parry, Ellwood C., III. *The Art of Thomas Cole: Ambition and Imagination*. Newark: University of Delaware Press, 1988.

———. "On the Outside Looking In: Thomas Cole as a Critic of American Culture," in *Thomas Cole: Drawn to Nature*. Albany: Albany Institute of History and Art, 1993.

Patterson, Jerry E. *The First Four Hundred*. New York: Rizzoli International Publications, 2000.

Peck, Amelia, ed.. *Lyndhurst: A Guide to the House and Landscape*. Tarrytown, New York: Lyndhurst, 1988.

———. *Alexander Jackson Davis: American Architect, 1803–1892*. New York: Rizzoli International Publications, 1992.

Peck, Amelia, and Carol Irish. *Candace Wheeler: The Art and Enterprise of American Design, 1875-1900*. New York: Metropolitan Museum of Art, 2001.

Phillips, Sandra S., and Linda Weintraub, eds. *Charmed Places: Husdon River Artists and Their Houses, Studios, and Vistas*. New York: Harry N. Abrams, 1988.

Pierson, Jr., William H. *American Buildings and Their Architects: The Colonial and Neo-Classical Styles*. Garden City, NY: Anchor Books, 1976.

Piwonka, Ruth. *A Portrait of Livingston Manor: 1686–1850*. Germantown, New York: Friends of Clermont, 1986.

Piwonka, Ruth, and Roderic H. Blackburn. *A Visible Heritage: Columbia County, New York, A History in Art and Architecure*. Kinderhook, NY: The Columbia County Historical Society, 1977.

Powell, Earl A. *Thomas Cole*. New York: Harry N. Abrams, 2000.

Reed, John. *The Hudson River Valley*. New York: Clarkson Potter, 1960.

Reiff, Daniel D. *Small Georgian Houses in England and Virginia: Origins and Development through the 1750's*. London and Toronto: University of Delaware Press and Associated University Presses, 1986.

———. *Houses from Books: Treatises, Pattern Books, and Catalogs in American Architecture, 1738–1950: A History and Guide*. University Park, PA: The Pennsylvania State University Press, 2000.

Reynolds, Helen Wilkinson. *Dutchess County Doorways, and Other Examples of Period Work in Wood, 1730–1830*. New York: William Farquhar Payson, 1931.

———. *Dutch Houses in the Hudson Valley Before 1776*. New York: Dover Publications, Inc., 1965.

Rice, Norman S., et al. *New York Furniture Before 1840 in the Collection of the Albany Institute of History and Art*. Albany: Albany Institute of History and Art, 1962.

Risk, Louise B. *House on the Hudson*. Privately published, 1993.

Root, Edward W. *Philip Hooker: A Contribution to the Study of the Renaissance in America*. New York: Charles Scribner's Sons, 1929.

Ryan, James Anthony. *Frederic Church's Olana: Architecture and Landscape as Art*. Hensonville, New York: Black Dome Press, 2001.

Sanchis, Frank. *American Architecture: Westchester County, New York.. Colonial to Comtemporary*. New York: North River Press, Inc. 1977.

Scherer, John L. *New York Furniture at the New York State Musuem*. Old Town Alexandria, VA: Highland House Publishers Inc., 1984.

Scully, Vincent. *New World Visions of Household Gods & Sacred Places: American Art, 1650-1914*. New York: Little, Brown and Company , 1988.

Selden, Ruth. "Architectural History of Philipse Manor Hall." Unpublished. New York State Department of Parks and Recreation, Division for Historic Preservation, 1976.

Shaver, Peter D. *The National Register of Historic Places in New York State*. New York: Rizzoli International Publications, 1993.

Smith III, Karl Beckwith. *Hudson Heritage: An Artist's Perspective on Architecture*. Cold Spring, NY: Salmagundi Press, 1989.

Smith, McKelden, ed. *The Great Estates Region of the Hudson River Valley*. Tarrytown, New York: Historic Hudson Valley Press, 1998.

Stein, Roger B. "Art as Ideology: The Aesthetic Movement in Its American Cultural Context" in Doreen Bolger Burke, ed., *In Pursuit of Beauty: Americans and the Aesthetic Movement*. New York: The Metropolitan Museum of Art, 1986.

Talman, Wilfred Blanch, and the Book Committee, Tappantown Historical Society. *Tappan: 300 Years, 1686–1986*. Tappan, New York: The Tappantown Historical Society, 1988.

Thomas Cole: Drawn to Nature. Albany, NY: Albany Institute of History and Art, 1993.

Tinterow, Gary X. Cornelius Wynkoop House, National Register of Historic Places Application.

Tomlan, Mary Raddant, in association with Ruth Osgood Trovato, eds., Douglas G. Bucher and W. Richard Wheeler, contributing authors. *A Neat Plain Modern Stile: Philip Hooker and His Contemporaries, 1796–1836*. Amherst, MA: University of Massachusetts Press, 1993.

Toole, R.M., Office of. Historic Landscape Report: James Vanderpoel House Property. Saratoga Springs, New York, 1994.

———. Landscape Research Report: Thomas Cole's Cedar Grove. Saratoga Springs, New York, 2002.

Tracy, Berry B. and Mary Black. *Federal Furniture and Decorative Arts at Boscobel*. Garrison, New York: Boscobel Restoration Inc.; New York: Harry N. Abrams, 1981.

Van Alen House: Historic Structure Report, 2001. Kinderhook, NY: The Columbia County Historical Society, 2001.

Van der Donck, Adriaen. *A Description of the New Netherlands*. Original Dutch edition, 1655. English translation originally published in the *Collections of the New-York Historical Society*. 2d ser., v. 1 (1841), p. [125]–242. Reprint, edited by Thomas F. O'Donnell. Syracuse, NY: Syracuse University Press, 1968.

Van Zandt, Roland. *Chronicles of the Hudson: Three Centuries of Travel and Adventure*. Hensonville, NY: Black Dome Press Corp., 1992.

Vaux, Calvert. *Villas & Cottages: The Great Architectural Style-Book of the Hudson River School*. New York: Harper, 1864. Reprint. New York: Dover Publications, Inc., 1970.

Vedder, J. Van Vechten. *Offical History of Greene County New York*. Cornwallville, NY: Hope Farms Press, 1985.

Waite, Diana S. *Ornamental Ironwork: Two Centuries of Craftsmanship in Albany and Troy, New York*. Albany, NY: Mount Ida Press, 1990.

Waite, Diana S., ed. *Albany Architecture*. Albany, NY: Mount Ida Press, 1993.

Whiffen, Marcus. *American Architecture: Volume 1, 1607–1860*. Cambridge, MA: The MIT Press, 1981.

White, Samuel G. *The Houses of McKim, Mead & White*. New York: Rizzoli International Publications, 1998.

Whitefield, Edwin. *Hudson River Houses: The Hudson River and Rail Road Illustrated*. New York: North River Press, Inc., 1981.

Wilstach, Paul. *Hudson River Landings*. New York: Tudor Publishing, 1937.

Wilton, Andrew, and Tim Barringer. *American Sublime: Landscape Painting in the United States, 1820-1880*. Princeton, NJ: Princeton University Press, 2002.

Zukowsky, John, and Robbe Pierce Stimson. *Hudson River Villas*. New York: Rizzoli International Publications, 1985.

Acknowledgments

For their support and advice, I wish to thank Joan Davidson and Mike Gladstone of Furthermore; Amy Facca; James Gold and Ruth Pierpont of the New York State Office of Parks, Recreation, and Historic Preservation; Scott Heyl and Jay DiLorenzo of the Preservation League of New York State; David Morton, Rizzoli; McKelden Smith, Historic Hudson Valley; Elizabeth White, project editor; and Abigail Sturges, who designed this beautiful book. Most grateful thanks to James Ivory for his elegant foreword.

Heartfelt thanks to Anne Skillion, in particular, for her editorial and scholarly assistance, and, for their partnership and much excellent information, Douglas Bucher; Fred Cawley, Rensselaer Polytechnic Institute; Tricia Fusco; John Kinnear; Celeste Kirton; Stephanie Mauri, Dutchess County Historical Society; Mary McLaughlin; Scott Newman; Joan Redmond; James Sexton; and Evelyn Trebilcock, Olana.

The following museums, historical societies and government agencies provided much assistance: Albany Institute of History and Art; Columbia County Historical Society; Dutchess County Historical Society; Greene County Historical Society; Historic Hudson Valley; Huguenot Historical Society; New York State Office of Parks, Recreation and Historic Preservation; Orange County Historical Society; Rensselaer County Historical Society; Tappantown Historical Society; and Ulster County Historical Society.

I wish to thank the following curators and site managers of the house museums for their cheerful assistance over the past two years: Charles Lyle, Boscobel; Raymond Beecher and Shelby Mattice, The Bronck Museum; Robert Henry Stackman, Jack Van Loan, and Elizabeth Jacks, Cedar Grove; Bruce Naramore, Clermont; Harold Jones, John De Wint House; Michael Clark and Nina Pierro, John Ellison House; Donna Hassler, Hart-Cluett House; Jane Kellar, Fred Johnston Museum; Susan Greenstein, Kykuit; Lesile LeFever, Locust Lawn; Susanne Pandich and Cathryn Anders, Lyndhurst; Lucy Kuriger, Montgomery Place; Linda McLean, Evelyn Trebilcock, and Sara Griffen, Olana; Heather Iannucci and Charles Casimiro, Philipse Manor Hall; Marcy Shaffer, Schuyler Mansion; Sarah Olsen and Anne Jordan, Springwood: FDR Historic Site; Melodye Moore and Susan Walker, Staatsburgh; Dina Friedman, Sunnyside; Brian Buff, Ten Broeck Mansion; Althea Corey, Van Cortlandt Manor; Laura Correa, Frederick Van Cortlandt House; Anne Jordan, Vanderbilt Mansion; and Sharon Palmer and Susan Tripp, James Vanderpoel House and Luykas Van Alen House.

For sharing their homes, thanks to the owners of the private houses in this book: Eliot and Susie Clarke; Nancy and Sébastien de La Selle; Martin and Meredith Dolan; Jane and Robert Hottensen; James Ivory and Ismail Merchant; Richard Jenrette; Robert Johnson; Gregory Long and Scott Newman; Norman Posner and Charles Baker; Zane Studenroth; John Szemansco; and Gary Tinterow.

Index

Page numbers in italics refer to illustrations and captions.

Illustration and Photo Credits

page 28 Robert Bolton, *History of the County of Westchester.*

page 32 Courtesy of Philipse Manor Hall

page 33 Benson J. Lossing, *The Hudson: From the Wilderness to the Sea.*

page 34, top Dwight James Baum, *Great Georgian Houses of America.*

page 34, below Edward Hagaman Hall, *Philipse Manor Hall at Yonkers, N.Y.*

pages 36, 42 Donald Millar, *Measured Drawings of Some Colonial and Georgian Houses.*

page 52 Helen Reynolds, *Dutch Houses in the Hudson Valley Before 1776.*

page 68 William Halfpenny, *The Modern Builders Assistant.*

page 86 Courtesy of Douglas Bucher.

page 95 Dwight James Baum, *Great Georgian Houses of North America.*

page 126 Wadsworth Atheneum, Hartford. Purchased through the gift of Henry and Walter Keney.

page 113 Roger Kennedy, *Orders from France.*

page 141 McKelden Smith, *The Great Estates Region of the Hudson River Valley.*

page 148 John G. Waite Associates, *The Marble House of Second Street: Biography of a Town House and Its Occupants.*

pages 156, 165, 170 Minard Lefever, *Modern Builder's Guide.*

page 188 The Metropolitan Museum of Art, Harris Brisbane Dick Fund, 1924 (24.66.70). Photograph © 1990.

page 195 Alexander Jackson Downing, *The Architecture of Country Houses.*

page 201 Collection at Olana. New York State Office of Parks, Recreation, and Historic Preservation.

page 208 Cooper-Hewitt, National Design Museum, Smithsonian Institution. Gift of Louis P. Church, 1917-4-582-c. Photograph by Ken Pelka

page 216 James Gibbs, *Book of Architecture.*

page 230 Courtesy of the author.

page 234 History American Buildings Survey, Library of Congress.

page 243 Courtesy of Historic Hudson Valley.